ALSO BY BURT HARDING

Hiding in Plain Sight

The Power of Awareness

The Fire & Mystery of Awareness

The Truth the World Doesn't Want You to Know

Set Your Heart Free Forever

The Wonder of You

The Four GROUND - BREAKING UNKNOWN *Facts of* REALITY

BURT V. HARDING

Balboa Press books may be ordered through booksellers or by contacting:

Balboa Press
A Division of Hay House
1663 Liberty Drive
Bloomington, IN 47403
www.balboapress.com
1 (877) 407-4847

Print information available on the last page.

ISBN: 978-1-9822-3494-2 (sc)
ISBN: 978-1-9822-3493-5 (e)

Balboa Press rev. date: 09/13/2019

Contents

I dedicate this book to my lovely daughter,
Debra Harding, who is a chip off the old block.

Also dedicated to my infinite partner, Suzy Johnston.

Author's Preface

Understand these Four Unknown Facts of Reality, and you will never think the same again.

This is how it happened. My daughter Debra, a meditation teacher and Reiki Master, decided to spend two weeks with me after a twenty-two-year absence. The meeting at the airport was prophetic.

We decided to do some video talks based on love without preparation, thoroughly spontaneously. In our fourth video, I blurted to YouTube viewers, "If you asked me what have I learned in forty years of spiritual work and service I would reply "nothing, but trust in the Spirit I AM." This triggered quite a few responses from viewers asking for greater clarification. Since my daughter was about to leave for her home in Ontario, I postponed the replies to these questions until I was alone and ready.

That evening, in bed, a "vision" of the answer appeared. I got up at 3 A.M. feeling an uncontrollable urge to write on the board Debra put up for me before she left. It was as if my hand started writing by itself. Before I knew what happened, the Four Ground-Breaking Facts were exposed. So uncompromisingly simple and clear, I felt temporarily stunned.

These Four Facts of Reality will answer every possible question about life. Anything the human mind can ask is clearly delineated in these four magnificent and clear-cut truths.

They will explain the seeming paradox of truth, the self-contradictions, the reason we sabotage ourselves, the fears we labor under, the emotional pains we keep repeating. Why the unrelenting frustrations of coming and going, the inability to have faith in our own true nature and, most of all, why we cannot comprehend simple, obvious truths about us.

For those ready and ripe individuals, these four facts are a great blessing. They are simplicity itself and make psychology, philosophy, metaphysics and all spiritual beliefs so clear that peace and faith are a natural result.

Introduction

One of the most obvious facts about our life is that we exist, and, we KNOW that we exist. We take our human beingness for granted and rarely ask *"what is a human?"* and *"what is a being?"* If we took the time to stop and LOOK at our life, we would be filled with wonder and the miracle of existence itself.

The central theme of this book is the simplicity of awakening to a life filled with peace and clarity. This book was prompted for this one simple purpose. By being human, we are in a perfect position to understand life and our place in it. There is nothing to be done in addition to being alive, except accepting life as it is without resisting or avoiding it. There is no preparation for life, no dress-rehearsal.

You are already alive and know you are alive. It's always here and now and waiting for you to make the choice to wake up.

The Four Unknown Ground-Breaking Facts do not propose an explanation of Reality for that would be absurd. Reality is infinite. What is required is LOOKING into the very process of life, and thus, waking up to its essence. This waking up to its essence arises spontaneously and naturally as the form of your very life.

Life is not to be figured out; it's not based on a reasoning process. It is its own explanation and immediately obviates the need for any other. It is a matter of being willing to LOOK at the miracle of Life itself.

The Miracle: Obviousness of Consciousness

No one, as of yet, has ever been able to understand consciousness, and no scientist, however brilliant, has ever been given a grant to explain it. There is no possible way that consciousness can ever be understood and yet consciousness is all there is! Everything seen and unseen is consciousness.

Pause for a moment to consider that consciousness was never born and therefore never dies.

Life is made up of consciousness. However, it does not stop there. It is also aware of itself. Amazing insights happen when we stop and LOOK at this mind-boggling truth!

I am awareness conscious of itself.

Some psychologists and even scientists have proposed that consciousness emerged from the brain. Awakening proves, beyond a doubt, that such a proposal is absurd. Dr. Eben Alexander, a neuroscientist, wrote books on the subject until one day he suffered brain death, Resuscitated, he feared becoming a mental vegetable. Yet, he emerged a brilliant man who proved consciousness exists beyond the brain writing a bestseller in forty languages titled, *Proof of Heaven*. He now lectures widely around the world that the brain is a filter of consciousness.

As you read with an open heart and mind, you will make discoveries that consciousness is, primarily, pure in itself, known as Pure Consciousness or Pure Awareness. This means that our very nature is beyond time as we know it and, also beyond space.

When in Canada, if you Skype someone in Germany or Australia, you both talk in the now-moment despite a different day and vast space. Doesn't this prove that "NOW" is beyond time and space? Doesn't it also prove that past and future are simultaneous and never truly *past* nor *future*? Can the mind understand this?

What is mind? What is thought? What is conscious awareness?

We all identify with thought and create our conditioned world by this law of attraction, yet how real is it when it's altered by thought itself?

Our daily life is run by thoughts, controlled by thoughts and acted by thoughts. And yet, we can stop and be aware of these thoughts. Do you see the implication of this simple process?

Did you know that the moment you see a thought as a thought, it shifts and changes?

The average human being sees thought as their reality the moment they believe that thought. Yet, belief and thought go hand-in-hand. A thought believed in produces your world.

Now here's a mind-boggling truth: a thought is a concept and never reality!

This is the law of attraction. The world we see is the world we have attracted, and yet it is only real to us. A concept is never real and yet the human lives in that world.

The word LOOKING implies the awareness of observing thought as a thought. Can you begin to see the wonder and power of this simple statement? Yet, this is an obvious fact and proven in an honest moment's effort.

Deepak Chopra said that we think an average of 26,000 thoughts a day. Do you wonder why so many people suffer anxiety, panic attacks, depression, fear, insanity, etc.? They are all produced by thought.

Now listen carefully. Pause and FEEL out the great wonder of these simple questions, "Who is thinking these thoughts?"

You will probably say "me." Okay fine. Now pause for a moment and answer the following: "Who is aware of these thoughts?"

Take your time before you answer.

It is NOT the "me" who is aware of these thoughts but awareness itself. The "me" is a fabrication of conditioned thought associated with a given name at birth, combined with memories of conditioned imagination. In other words, everything that is conditioned cannot be real except through belief. Do you see this clearly?

Therefore, who is aware of these thoughts?

It can't be your name or conditioned mind but the AWARENESS YOU ARE!

In other words, what is real about you?

Is it that which changes, shifts and alters such as conditioning or the awareness beyond time and space?

Here's your first bit of relief. You are the very awareness of consciousness itself. Thus, when you shed your body, your BEING is set free from time and space and thus lives in the state of total UNCONDITIONAL LOVE.

If this is hard to grasp at this moment, that's perfectly okay, because as you go on with the FOUR GROUND-BREAKING FACTS, all this will be revealed to you.

This book will trigger your awakening simply with your honest and sincere LOOKING.

Right now, say to yourself, "I am sincere in wanting to know who I am!"

Spiritual-Sleep

Everyone is awareness, and yet almost no one notices awareness itself. This lack of knowing awareness and accepting it without exploration is known as "spiritual sleep," or the "veil."

The average person is so asleep to who and what they are that the Russian Sage Gurdjieff said, "The average person talks, walks and experiences as if awake on the outside, but inside he is snoring."

As a youngster, I was deeply lonely, shy and unhappy. I was brought up in a primitive religion that believed we are all born in sin and punished if we don't obey the rules of conditioned society and its religion. I was taught about the devil, hell, and damnation. I was also taught that sex was a sin, and yet as a youngster, I explored sexuality with gusto always believing I am going to hell for being a bad kid. As we skinny-dipped in the warm Summer waters of the ocean, we all believed we were going to hell for this adventure. Later, even as a youngster I witnessed as we grew into adulthood, we all felt bad about ourselves. This belief damaged our self-esteem despite our pretended bravado and carried with it the belief, "I am not good enough."

The belief as a young man was, "I didn't ask to be born!" and yet here I am.

Consciousness was not something I possessed, but it was who I AM. My appearance was simply how consciousness "decided" to appear in order to evolve itself into the Being that was already perfect Love. My "job" on earth was and is this discovery of my glory. This clarity came to me much, much later in life during a Light experience. But I am getting ahead of myself. All this you will come to know. Keep mind and heart open.

Awakening to the true life is simple if we are willing to choose what is good, true and loving. You will discover, through your earnest reading, that you are a wonderful Being. We have a choice between love or fear. Fear is often chosen by the conditioned response to acquired beliefs. However, our capacity to know who we are is very simple. Just listen to this . . .

You are all that is good and loving.

If you were to honestly ask your heart while depressed, "How would I rather feel than this depression?" immediately your heart will respond (if you are honest with yourself), "I would rather feel good."

Why? Very simple. It is because your true nature is pure consciousness, which is also known as the heavenly state of being.

Your true nature is goodness, and your expression is love.

Separation from Reality

I have been involved in hypnotherapy for thirty years and have had hundreds of clients. Through these encounters, I have noticed, unmistakably, that the only problem is one and the same—separation from Reality. In other words, believing in the idea of a personal self that gets hurt, abandoned, threatened and abused.

In the latter years, I "received" inner guidance that therapy doesn't work in the conventional sense because the ego is addressed as a reality. As a result of this insight, I changed the name hypnotherapy to SuperSentience. It's a method where only awareness of one's true nature is necessary. It is this awareness alone, once allowed in our consciousness, where lasting healing happens. *A Course in Miracles* calls it Atonement.

Allowing Awareness of our true Being!

Once we allow awareness of our true Being in its true form, without condition, then there is permanent change. From this perspective, something comes into existence only when it enters our field of awareness. Once we are aware of something, we will inevitably think, act and feel from it.

"I" did not write this book in the sense of Burt writing a book. It happened despite me. I couldn't resist it any more than I could resist going to the bathroom. It just took over! I sat down and wrote it only to look forward to continuing it until my Spirit was finished with it. This is what I'm doing now as you read these words. I feel that if I can connect with you, something will happen to trigger your awareness of the wonder that you really are.

So many people have asked me, "But what if I'm not ready to awaken yet? After all, I've been reading this stuff for a long time?"

There is nothing that gets you stuck more than the idea you are not ready. In fact, the moment the ego is challenged, we back off and think, "I think I'm not ready!" but it is only ego fear talking.

Your entire existence has been the preparation for this moment you are now living. The fact that you are now reading this book is proof enough you are ready. Nothing happens by chance. All that is necessary is for you to consciously surrender at this moment. You are always ready for life, truth, and God. You were born to discover this wonderful truth.

Famous author, Eckhart Tolle, of *The Power of Now,* explained how he spontaneously woke up. The following excerpt was taken from the old *Shared Vision* article Sept. 2000 issue:

"Until the late twenties, depression, acute anxiety, and thoughts of suicide characterized his adulthood. Then one night he said, 'I can't live with myself any longer.' Uttering this sentence a few times gave him pause. He thought: 'Who is the self that I can't live with, and who am I?'"

And with this, Tolle says he broke his attachment to his negative thinking and his identification with his thoughts.

"My sense of I was no longer trapped in the unhappy me," says Tolle. The "I" stood back and looked at the whole structure of unhappiness and the heaviness of that. The withdrawal from identification with that was so complete that the unhappy self crumbled as if he pulled a plug out of an inflatable toy.

We are always ready for spiritual work because it is our true nature of happiness and love. What prevents us is our belief that we are not ready, our belief that there is something still to achieve, and our belief that we must attain some knowing prior to beginning. Our belief that we are not ready is a rationale for searching, for avoiding the inevitable.

You are ready when you are willing to wake up, and not when some external condition is met.

At this moment, as you read this, you have everything you need. All that is required is that you accept it without reservation.

The Four Ground-Breaking Facts

The average person has no clue to the Reality of these Four Facts. They are called "facts" because that's exactly what they are. They are our constant and never-changing Reality, and they are us this very moment. Science is beginning to understand these great truths.

We are all guided through Infinite Intelligence (ACIM calls it Holy Spirit). Breathtaking beauty awaits each one of us if we but allow ourselves to surrender to this vast unknown Source that created us, and, IS us!

This great truth of the Four Facts is not a teaching but rather a pointer to what we are failing to recognize—who we are.

These Four Facts are the Absolute Truth that escapes the average awareness due to the belief we are separate human beings. It is this very unawareness that has created all the chaos, suffering and emotional pain inherent in humanity. The question might arise, "Why is it like this?" "Why should there be suffering if Reality is perfect?"

It is the awareness of how things truly are that changes drastically the perspective of suffering.

Could it be that we are misperceiving what is real?

Could it be that we have a mistaken identity of who we are and thus, in that mistaken identity, believe we are suffering?

This knowing of these Four Unknown Facts is not only the way things truly are, but upon awakening to their reality you realize, "How else could it be if life is good?"

Once you become aware of these Four Facts of Reality and see their truth in daily life, then you are clear, free, liberated and fulfilled.

The First GROUND-BREAKING Unknown *Fact of* Reality

There is Only Emptiness

The most important fact of Reality is this: there is only EMPTINESS! Buddha emphasized this fact but was greatly misunderstood. EMPTINESS has no actual word to describe it!

It is nothingness or no-thingness. It is boundless space. It is the great void from which all things emerged. Another example we can relate to, at least intellectually, is electricity. Electricity is simply space, void, emptiness and yet when harnessed through positive and negative wiring we can utilize it. Electricity comes from the word electron which is the nucleus of the atom—space or nothingness.

In *A Course in Miracles,* we read, "I am Spirit." In other words, we are not who we think we are. We are emptiness. In fact, we are an infinite being.

What is the nature of this Emptiness? Obviously, it's pure awareness otherwise how can it create, out of itself, conscious beings? This pure awareness, although beyond any definition, is also bliss. Yogis call it sat-chit-ananda. It is pure joy and love from which all goodness emerges. This joy can be witnessed in puppies, kittens and little children. This is the natural state before thought enters and identifies with its beliefs. This is when pure awareness creates thought out of itself and becomes consciousness. When you look into your own eyes in a mirror for a long time, you will begin to catch a glimpse of this nothingness. Sincerely and honestly inquire, as you look into your own eyes, and ask, "Who am I?"

"Who is it really that is behind these eyes?"

"Is there anybody home?"

"Could it be just the void appearing as my personality and body?"

After all, everything changes including our bodies and yet

the one who is witnessing all of this since childhood has not changed one iota. Who is the one who knows we have a body, who can say, "I think and I know I think."

"Who is aware of the thought?"

"Isn't it awareness itself?"

A Course in Miracles, "Miracles reawaken the awareness that the Spirit, is not the body, is the altar of Truth. This is the recognition that leads to the healing power of the miracle."

In Truth, there is only Spirit, Energy, The Great Void or Emptiness. Can the mind understand this nothingness? It is impossible for the mind to grasp such direct and subtle simplicity. Yet, how can we comprehend it if not through the mind? This is where it gets interesting.

As we learn to observe our thoughts, we will eventually discover that our whole world is a creation of our thoughts (perceptions, ideas, viewpoints, beliefs), and yet we can be aware of these thoughts.

Who is the one who is aware? (Repeating since this is the most important fact.) So, we need not even understand but simply grasp the fact that we are emptiness observing its created activity.

Remember the following great truths:

You are either functioning from the idea of thought or emptiness.

Thought is the past ego-idea.

Emptiness is bliss, fulfillment and true love.

To feel this statement, notice that you think, *and*, you are aware of the thought.

Who is aware of the thought?

Feel it out! No one is aware of the thought because it is emptiness. <u>It is emptiness that observes</u>.

Starting to Wake Up

The moment we start recognizing the fact, through observation, that we are not the mental activity but the void itself, we develop detachment. Through this detached observation, we learn this incredible and freedom-giving truth:

We are NOT these conditioned beliefs and thoughts; we are the emptiness observing it.

Can you imagine the freedom and peace that comes from this simple truth? Fears will begin to drop so rapidly you will wonder how you could have lived before in such unawareness!

Any scientist knows that ENERGY IS INDESTRUCTIBLE, simply changing form. Consciousness is intelligent indestructible energy that has never known time. IT JUST IS!

When I had my first Light Experience in 2006 at the hospital accompanied with my then-wife Sivia, the simplicity, beauty and unconditional love that is pure consciousness crushed upon me with such amazement and even shock, I wondered how such glory and beauty was missed by the vast majority when the whole world cries for a taste of this heavenly love and bliss. Yet, believe it or not, I was forced by doctors and nurses NOT to talk about it lest I be fingered as a schizophrenic or borderline psychotic. It was a sobering fact that most people have no idea who they are or how amazingly beautiful they are in truth. And, because of this unawareness, most people suffered deep emotional pain, anxiety and panic attacks and bursts of anger and fear were commonplace.

When I tried to communicate my experience, I was met with a trance-like look of either disbelief or simply "so what!"

I learned how the ordinary conditioned mind simply couldn't fathom the glory that lies within their very consciousness.

I didn't talk about it for over eleven years now that IANDS

has become popular. (International Association of Near Death Studies)

Awareness in its pure state is the highest bliss of unconditional love, yet the mind is so active, so undisciplined and wayward that no chance is given oneself to experience its bliss.

Repeating, pure awareness is an intelligent indestructible energy that has never known time or space, and that's why when people experience near-death they are transformed by their out-of-body emptiness. I have studied these cases for two years with the IANDS organization.

Once there is the direct experience of emptiness in its true natural state, then one is never the same after. The taste of unconditional love cleanses the subconscious from its past ego-conditioned fears and phobias. The fear of physical death is wiped out. In its place is a peace that never goes away.

Emptiness also known as Spirit, nothingness or fullness, appears as human form in order to experience itself. Our journey in human form is to directly experience life as it happens without running away from it. It's in this facing of our worst fears that we also awaken to our potential unconditional love. Eckhart Tolle is a case in point of sudden awakening to this seeing of the truth.

Name and form are essential for the evolution of consciousness expansion, which is also known as the awareness of itself. In simpler terms, see that you are not the thought, nor the conditioned mind, but the awareness of it without attachment to it.

This is the play of consciousness while on earth subjected to time and space. This play" of consciousness which appears real, is also known as the content of consciousness normally called "mind."

The Universe we see and experience as real is all mind. Robert Adams, a fully enlightened Western Master, put it this way, "The realization that everything you see, the Universe, people, insects, worms, the mineral kingdom, the vegetable kingdom, your body, your mind, everything that appears, is a manifestation of your mind."

Buddha and Bhagavan Ramana Maharshi said exactly the same thing. Jesus pointed to the fact that although he was in the world yet, he was not of it. He also referred to the Pure Consciousness as the Father. He said, "In my Father's House there are many mansions." Mansions mean dimensions and levels of seeing-experiencing.

Being Aware of Thoughts as Thoughts

What you think about all day determines your emotional feelings and your world. Thought is attractive, and the LAW OF ATTRACTION is the law of mind. This means that how you see the world is exactly how you think about it. And, it is only real to you. Here is a scoop: the world you see is your mind precisely!

If you fear something; if you worry; if you believe something is wrong somewhere; if you think you are suffering from lack or limitation, or sickness anytime, then be aware that you are out of alignment with Source energy. The healing of this is very simple. Just see this is all a manifestation of your mind because in truth you are empty.

Keep reminding yourself that you are an empty vessel (pure awareness by nature). This empty vessel is unconditional love. When a child looks at you with his sweet, adorable eyes and is laughing, he simply loves you because he is an empty vessel. He is not trying to figure you out; he is not trying to make sense; he is not hoping you love him in return. He simply loves you unconditionally.

The conditioned mind separates you from people by creating an appearance that seems real. This appearance is an energy field that is immediately felt by others. What is real is not the content of consciousness but consciousness itself. No matter how old you are, in your true state you are an innocent child. Thinking that what you sense is real is a habit of your conditioned mind.

You do not deny your mind and thinking but, simply LOOK at yourself as an empty vessel containing only pure seeing. You are "just here."

This question is bound to arise, "But can we help buying into this play of consciousness?"

Not really! It's to be resolved that only your pure nature can keep you aligned with Source and so, you don't control anything or resist anything, but simply LOOK (be aware) and know that you are temporarily caught, and it's okay.

SMILE! And know that this is all evolution—the awakening process to the truth of Being.

It is all consciousness-evolution like the child learning to walk is bound to fall, but it's all okay. This is the process of learning. It is the full acceptance of whatever the Universe dishes out, and then seeing it as a lesson to be learned. HOW? By smiling the moment you become aware you're caught, and it's okay. This is enough to keep you opening your heart and loving yourself.

We are daily bombarded by ways and means to make us happy, fulfilled people and yet nothing works except your attitude of wanting only consciousness-evolution. How often we entertain the thought of making lots of money to bring us happiness; or buying new gadgets, playthings to keep us occupied and yet nothing works to make you a fulfilled human being except consciousness-evolution.

Consciousness Evolution

Be determined to evolve consciously with every seeming setback or problem. Ram Dass used to say, "All problems are grist for the mill!" This means that everything that happens you rather didn't is a test of your spiritual stamina. Use every slight concern, worry or fear as a challenge to growth in emptiness also known as Presence.

When Ramana Maharshi would look directly at a student, the student would feel it all over. The empty look was often enough to trigger recognition in the student.

How to Empty Yourself

It is very simple to empty yourself. Smile, take a deep breath and be-here-now!

This NOW moment is reality because the past is gone and the future not yet. However, what is more than this explanation of time is that TIME ITSELF is only real to the conditioned mind (linear brain). Your true Source is unborn, undying, timeless, infinite and eternal. Therefore, if a problem is troubling you and you enter this moment through emptiness, then the solution will arise by itself through emptiness. How?

When a money problem arises then, I simply give it to emptiness, and it has never failed to resolve itself. How does it do it? To tell you the truth I really don't know. But it has always worked, and I have never been wanting.

Entering emptiness is a stillness and in that stillness lies great power. In fact, the greatest seven words in the English language are . . .

BE STILL AND KNOW I AM GOD!

Through that stillness, we become aware of our eternal nature since time-consciousness begins to fall away. We come to know this greatest of lessons, "This is all there is!" It is the holy instant.

Awareness comes from the "one consciousness" and isn't limited to name and form but plays the part as if it is. You can say "my body" or "my mind," but you can't say "my awareness" because awareness doesn't belong to anyone.

AWARENESS IS!

This pure awareness is what we call God or the Light of unconditional love often referred to as the heavenly state of Being. Heaven is not a place but a state of being, empty. So, people who have experienced a near-death experience (and who have actually died and were resuscitated again) tell of a state that words cannot convey. They tell of a feeling of love that they never knew existed. In fact, they didn't want to be resuscitated because that "place" of Being was their true Home.

When I experienced the Light of Unconditional Love in the hospital, I learned more in that timeless minute than I had my entire past life. It took over eleven years not talking about it, for no one understood. Yet, those who experienced this Light were never the same. Also, they had the feeling that words could never convey what the heart lucidly experienced. No one, from the millions who have experienced NDE, has ever forgotten their true Home of eternal joy and love.

One may ask, "Can we know what this Unconditional Love is like without having a Light experience?"

The answer is "YES," and that's why this book was written. I kept this feeling inside me for over eleven years without revealing what I actually experienced. I have researched it for two consecutive years and listened to many speakers from IANDS talking about their own experience of this unconditional LOVE. There are many such associations spreading throughout the world. There is one in your city also.

What is this experience and why does it bring transformation? Our true nature is emptiness beyond time and space. Thus, when the body is shed temporarily then our EMPTINESS also called "soul" or "Spirit" lives in timeless essence. What is left is pure awareness which is the highest joy and love. Yet, our memories, personality, emotions are intact but never negative. Negativity exists only in time and space known as earth time.

Earth Time Consciousness

Why do we need to live in this world if it is filled with suffering?

The word "suffering" is a misconception brought about by the confinement of time and space. However, it's felt as suffering because we are not willing to acknowledge our birthright as pure awareness.

For example, when you are aware of anything, who is being aware?

When you sincerely LOOK into who is really being aware, you will experience the first shock of awakening. No one is being aware! There is just awareness! It is all emptiness known as pure Being. This pure being is itself the love, joy, peace and heavenly bliss we seek without realizing it. And, it is when we recognize how we seek unconditional love all the time that we get another shock of awakening. This unconditional love is the real meaning of HOME!

The Continual Seeking of Unconditional Love

Here is your second awakening shock. Listen carefully and do not merely accept it because I am saying it. Look into it. Feel it with your whole heart.

This is the shocking statement that will awaken your Spirit. You are seeking unconditional love all the time!

Picture a boy constantly yelled at by his mother for not behaving as he should. The more she yells at him, the more he retreats into his shell, becoming even more difficult to reach. What is happening?

If we were to enter the boy's real feeling, it's this, "Mommy, why can't you love me as I am instead of the way you want me to be."

When we fall in love with someone, we crave special love. We want to be special in the eyes of our beloved. We want to own that love in order to feel complete. Thus, two lovers unite in that same need, "Love me unconditionally no matter how I act!"

In our religions, we thought that God loved us conditionally, that is, only when we behaved rightly and according to the rules. We couldn't conceive of God as being unconditional love, never judging us. In fact, we were taught that unless we didn't sin we couldn't enter heaven. This was the creation of man's law, and that's why religions never fully work—because they are based on control and guilt.

Krishnamurti, a great Master, considered as a world teacher, emphatically said that Truth is a pathless land. It needs no religion, no study, no rules but simply awakening to the truth of our Being nature.

How Do We Seek Unconditional Love?

Are you ready for another shock of your life? Are you ready to see the truth of this question?

Are you willing to be open to this revelation?

The answer is this: you are seeking unconditional love every time you rebel, yell, scream, slam doors, shout, feel hurt, rejected, unwanted, angry, upset, feel betrayed. Every negative reaction is an unconscious need, a cry for unconditional love.

The married man who strays, the married woman who feels betrayed, cheated and every child who feels unwanted and unloved is nothing more than a heart's cry for our true Home of unconditional love.

Are you willing to look at your personal hurt as a need for unconditional love? Yet, is it possible to get unconditional love from someone unawakened?

Waking up is very simple. It's the realization of unconditional love, which is, our true home. It's the realization of emptiness that can reveal our true home of unconditional love.

The word GOD is the epitome of that love that never judges, never controls, never scolds you or tells you how you should be but simply loves you because that is or true home. This is the Truth of our Being. And, emptiness will reveal the innocence of our true heart.

As you read this, you might feel that it is impossible in this world to love unconditionally. You are right if you think of yourself as merely a separate personal self without emptiness.

Emptiness is not difficult at all. Just sit still for a moment. Take a deep breath and say:

Now for just a few minutes, I will shed all fears, problems, worries and concerns to the wind. I am here and now without a past. I shed my identity as Mary, John or Burt, and just be here. I have no conceptions. I am not reaching for a solution. I have no expectations. I am just here empty—completely empty! Now I look and see nothing is left but this moment. I am now an empty vessel.

After having done that, just be totally honest with yourself, how did you feel? Didn't you feel complete without wanting anything? Didn't you feel happy? And best of all, didn't you feel love for yourself? Of course, you did!

This is what it means to love YOU! And this love is so innocent, so ripe, so pure that everyone you will look at is also an extension of YOU!

Emptiness is the True Love of Self

In non-duality teachings, it is often emphasized that there is no person, no individual and therefore there is no doer to do anything. There was a time, prior to my experience in the Light, to extinguish myself and thus be in the background. Although it didn't hurt me or sadden me, it didn't make me feel free and expressive.

The Light experience, on the other hand, gave me the freedom to be myself and not to be other than who I AM. In short, I effortlessly relaxed into my Being. It was a matter of allowing emptiness to be the Light I loved and surrendered to.

The Secret of Loving Yourself

Remember that neither the Internet, counselors, therapists or any psychology or philosophy have ever told you the secret of loving yourself. Chances are you were told how to improve yourself or how to be more charming and magnetic, but, who has ever told you how AMAZING you really are, even at this moment reading this? You are amazing because you are not an object bound to time and space but a BEING totally empty, and thus pure energy. Only a few years ago, if we were told we could Skype it would have seemed unbelievable. We are entering the fifth dimension of consciousness. Both Gaia (our planet) and ourselves are advancing at break-neck speed toward the unlimited possibilities of going beyond time and space.

In years to come, we will see wonders that can boggle our mind and even imagination.

We will see that even physical transportation by sea, air, and car will become obsolete when we enter the full knowing of our true nature as ENERGY—Emptiness. We could transport from one place to another as swiftly as sending an e-mail or calling someone on your mobile phone.

Many have said, "I find it easy to love people but difficult to love myself!" First of all, you cannot love another if you don't love yourself. Loving yourself is the first requisite, without which you are ever lost in a mad world of thoughts and emotions that seem so very real.

What Does It Mean to Love Yourself?

It is to see that you are literally empty, that the body is only a shell of consciousness, an object necessary to find the truth of yourself. When you see yourself as you actually are (Spirit-Energy) then the possibilities of love are endless.

First of all, you are never really hurt by insults, demeaning people and comments or aggression against you. Who can hurt an empty vessel?

Secondly, as you discover your unlimited being, you will feel impelled, if not compelled, to help and guide others lovingly because you see everyone as part of you.

Third, life will stop being a "problem" and become an unending lesson for your growth, because, you will see clearly, that all emotional pain is a seeking of unconditional love.

Fourth, you will feel charged like a battery towards everything that happens to you as just more lessons to learn of unending love.

Fifth, we stop being victims of our thoughts and emotions and find lasting peace.

And sixth, you'll discover that only goodness, love, peace, joy and fulfillment are real.

You are AMAZING

Even as you read this, the possibilities are endless. The start of these wonders will begin when you REALIZE you're not an object but Spirit-Energy of immense potential. You start your great life with your recognition of Spirit-Emptiness and then move into possibilities even beyond imagination. Anything is possible when you really know who you are.

Nowadays there are millions of people who leave their bodies and travel around endless space of the Universe. Then return to tell us the adventure. I know some people who do this as a matter of fact. These are people who've discovered the truth of their Being and are free agents without being caught in moralistic religious values but know, beyond doubt, that LOVE (unconditional love) rules the realm of Spirit.

How to Be Empty

This first ground-breaking fact is emptiness, and unless we start seeing how empty we are, we can never feel FULL! Sounds contradictory? Yes, because spiritual reality seems like a paradox. The reason is simple. We look at an objective world and make it so real that our very Spirit that created it in the first place is forgotten, even ignored. This is the great mistake that causes so much unnecessary pain and suffering.

Why do we look forward to sleep at night when we have had an active grueling day? Did you know that our spirit leaves our body at night and learns necessary lessons? We are not aware of this because we have never explored our true nature.

Have you ever got up in the morning feeling paralyzed physically and felt inwardly panicking? This is more common when the Spirit is not properly aligned with the physical form. This happens during sleep when suddenly awakened, and the Spirit hasn't had a chance to re-enter the physical form. It is this Spirit-Emptiness that makes you seem alive in your body.

Have you ever seen a dead body? All animation had left. What you saw was just a shell.

Simply believing we are objective forms causes all suffering in this world. We spend so much energy and time on our body that we forget who and what we actually are. When we look at a beautiful looking human being without character or Spirit-Energy then soon our attraction shifts.

There are Two Kinds of Emptiness

There is physical emptiness through false values that eventually becomes disgusting or real EMPTINESS that is sheer potential of unlimited possibilities. This latter value is what we are after. All physical radiance, real magnetism, attractive smile, and eyes are derived from Spirit-essence known as Emptiness.

In truth, you are not a human-doing but a human being. Human being simply means pure Spirit.

People often ask, "I don't know what to do with my life?"

"What is the best thing for me to do?"

"What is my purpose?"

These are questions asked because of a need to run, escape, avoid and resist the Spirit-Emptiness. When you fall in love with Spirit-Emptiness (which is your true Self), then all such questions fall away like leaves in Autumn.

Despite the fact that there are no real answers to these questions, the ego keeps trying. Why? The ego is deadly afraid of Spirit Energy because it's not something you can hold in your hand like an object. It is ephemeral and ineffable. The conditioned mind is afraid of anything it doesn't understand. Thus, if you are reading this and feel inspired, then congratulations, because this inspiration means in-Spirit.

If, on the other hand, you ask, "What am I supposed to do?

"What is my purpose?"

These are excuses not to entertain the truth of your being but rather escape it. BEING doesn't seek or do. Being loves itself just Being. In fact, in moments of great stillness and non-doing comes a resurgence that takes over without you realizing it.

I do not write these books but simply feel the inspiration that moves me and thus see my hand typing words that are in my heart. This is not planned ahead of time, and it all happens by itself through my Spirit force.

What precedes thought is pure feeling (emptiness felt as peace and bliss). If we intellectually interpret pure feeling as emptiness, then we create the thought of something as missing. Emptiness is not a void of feeling but rather an alive beingness, radiance, inspiration, an aliveness. Such a state of Being can never be bored, listless, tired or fed-up. It is ever creative because the emptiness is like a vast ocean of possibilities.

Pure awareness, emptiness, Spirit, etc. are pure feeling. Pure feeling means there are no thoughts how things should be. This inner silence is known as peace, harmony, love and bliss. This is our true natural state. If, however, we develop a NEED for these feelings then the opposite happens—our very need becomes their destruction. You cannot need what you already are. You do not develop these qualities; they are already you as emptiness. To be empty, you simply allow it by BEING.

Take a deep breath, smile inwardly, and look at a tree or sky or clouds or birds, etc.

Remember this: we do not do anything. Our purpose is simply to be. It is the BEING (emptiness) that will act through us and does what is best for us. It is this Being which is known as love, which does everything through us. Love does it all! Do you think that Albert Einstein, Mother Theresa or Albert Schweitzer planned what to do? Or, were they driven from the heart?

If you can tell the difference between ego decisions and following your heart, you have already taken a giant leap in consciousness.

When people are out of work what do they do? They usually look for a job to earn money! Can you realize this incredible waste of energy and "time?" However, if you know where your love is and follow it then you have "secured your future."

Benefits of "Learning" to Be

What if someone told you, "You need do nothing. Just 'Be.'" Can you imagine the questions, confusions and even anger at such a statement? Yet, it is the truth.

When I was a physiotherapist in Toronto, I worked hard and did enjoy the work. However, my boss wanted me to sell services to the executives that belonged to our exclusive club, to renew their expensive annual membership. This was done by playing tennis, golf and other games with them and losing even if I was better than they were. This was a ploy of my employer to make the members feel good and rejoin. After a while this got tedious, and I felt like a phony. All my enthusiasm for my work lost its attractiveness and I began to feel bad about myself. It led to eventual depression.

One day, in 1973 while getting ready to go to work I experienced a vision of a rather elderly gentleman. His face was crystal clear. His eyes penetrated mine like I never experienced before. His words were telepathically received without his mouth moving. His message was clear that I needed a different occupation. This experience stayed with me for over six months. When I was walking along with my date, I noticed a new spiritual bookstore. Upon entering, I spotted a picture of the man that appeared to me earlier. The book was *The Life and Teachings of Bhagavan Ramana Maharshi*.

I became transfixed as I held the book so that even the lady with me remarked, "What is wrong?" My hands trembled, and I shook inside feeling convinced that this message was real and meant for me. I took the book home (and still have it) and read it all in one night without sleeping. By morning I was convinced to quit my position as a physiotherapist and simply give my life to meditation and contemplative work. My boss was livid, to say the least. I walked out feeling free and happy with no goals or prospects for the future. I rented a bachelor basement apartment on Meighen Avenue with an Italian family. My one bedroom basement apartment was huge, and I retired hanging pictures all over of Bhagavan Ramana Maharshi.

I started doing Yoga asanas to keep in shape. The rest of the time I read, meditated, prayed and chanted his name. It all came naturally. One day while doing asanas a man spotted me and asked me if I would be interested in teaching yoga at the YMCA. In those days, Yoga was unknown, but soon I was having several classes a week. This led to CBC "Food for Thought" program where I was interviewed regarding Yoga and my classes. The response from phone calls and letters (there were no e-mail nor computers in those days) were overwhelming, and I was asked to attend another longer interview. This led to a CFTO TV series on the mind/body connection. Before I knew what was happening, I had a gathering of students and a company called the Unitrust Foundation.

I wrote my first book, *Be Aware – Be Free*, and advertised on TV. It sold well. My life took off from then on until I arrived in Vancouver after my TV series ended.

Now, why have I told you my story? I wanted to prove to

you that when I decided to "be" in my acquired new love, then Spirit took over and guided me. Many things have happened since then, and I never planned. I never planned my talks nor my writings. They just happened through inspiration (in Spirit).

All the great Masters tell us "to be." The unawareness of our inner potential is stifled by the ego's plans and efforts when not created by love through the heart of Being.

When we allow ourselves to be empty, a whole new world opens. It's as if we're breathing fresh air for the first time. We feel we are living effortlessly, confidently and securely. The things we wanted in our heart come to us. We become abundant, creative, inspired, and feel totally "lived" by a power that is our very life and is indescribable. It is as if we are taken over by a higher power, and that's the trust that awakens when we recognize our true nature as Emptiness. Worry becomes a thing of the past. Fear of the future is gone and so is insecurity. Love and joy become our normal expression. Effort "to do" is replaced by allowing it TO BE DONE. Our health improves, our energy doubles and even age takes a backseat.

We live in a world of strong ego that wants control and "doing" is not only the norm but anything else is considered downright lazy and irresponsible. And, here's the paradox: the reason we become lazy and irresponsible is because our "doing" becomes so heavy that we succumb to the stress. Stress always leads to distress and disease of mind or body or both.

Life was never meant to be a struggle, but a joy. Life isn't a problem to be solved but love to be released. You will eventually see that this is the most practical, most creative, most vitalizing way to live.

Be Empty with Your Humanness

When you allow yourself to be empty with your humanness you have become an integrated human being. Why? Simply because you are allowing LIFE to live through you. You trust the divine infinite intelligence and give it priority in your life. Thus, you begin to live from it. Here, both the human and the Being become one. It's this oneness that's relevant, the answer to everything which does all the work.

When we become aware of the human part's limitation, we become aware of higher possibilities that become our Feeling/ Knowing.

When Ishvara became enlightened, he was asked about his experience. His answer was,

"The experience of awakening has involved a deepening of what I call "feeling/knowing." It is not conceptual. It is something deeper, and, it is very exact. Feeling-Knowing is so apparent that it 'just is' and there is no doubt. It is not static, though. Feeling/Knowing keeps adding to itself, continually becoming more expansive. Feeling/Knowing is an awareness of the One Consciousness. The One Consciousness is my term for the word 'God' or 'Absolute.' These latter terms have parameters to them. Yet, my experience of the One Consciousness is that it has no parameter. It is the All-That-Is, and it is also nothingness. It is everything. Each individual is a unique experience and expression of the One. So, in essence, you are the One Consciousness experiencing itself as you. Each individual is an expression of the One Consciousness, but not separate. Each is a unique expression of the One Consciousness that is all of Life."

This Oneness or integration of the human-being, where the human and the being are united as one, is itself the whole experience of the peace, love, and freedom we have sought for centuries. It's the allowing, accepting, sense flowing part of being united with the human. There

is no sense of wrong or right, good and evil, should or shouldn't. There is only what-is.

Explore now as you listen to this about the negative feelings you have. What are negative feelings? Aren't they the resistance to being?

It's the human combating the "being." Now, can you feel how comforting, how relaxing, how freeing and joyous unity can be without the separation of human and being?

The Hard-Won Lesson: It's All Source

In our search for understanding and meaning, we are faced with a variety of approaches, studies, groups, religions, philosophies, beliefs, and a tremendous number of books. Often, we are confused with seemingly different teachings.

How can I know the real teaching when there are so many versions?

Throughout history, the real teachings given to us by Masters were controlled and manipulated by Popes and political leaders. When Jesus walked the earth, he was one of the real great Masters, but soon his pure teachings were corrupted to control the people through fear and guilt.

Jesus said, "The works that I do shall you also do," and emphasized, "The Kingdom of God is within you."

Yet, when he emphasized that only through Christ shall you enter heaven, it meant only through Christ-consciousness can you enter Heaven. Christ consciousness is the same as Unconditional Love. Bhagavan Ramana Maharshi was Christ-conscious and in fact, so are all awakened human beings. Yet, it was interpreted as only through faith in Jesus can one be saved, which is not true. The New Testament which initially contained the real teachings of Jesus were mostly removed. It left a big gap of eighteen years missing from Jesus' life.

Jesus waited until the late 1960's, when people were more ready to know the truth, giving us *A Course in Miracles*.

Jesus chose an elderly Jewish atheistic woman psychologist at Columbia University to receive the teaching. She declined it in the beginning, but soon the Voice wouldn't let go until it was finished. It took seven years' dictation before it was published.

I taught the *Course* in Vancouver and had large crowds of people in the late 80's. Yet, I found they were turning it into another belief system like a religion. I quit teaching it and resorted to Satsangs.

How can I know what is real?

By getting to know yourself and your pure awareness which is in every living being. When our consciousness is purified from its many beliefs about life and oneself, then one is left empty. It is this emptiness that is the truth of Being.

How can emptiness teach me the truth?

Just be still and listen to your natural state. Ask yourself, "What is it I want more than anything else in the world?" and you will "hear" the answer as surely as you are now breathing. What you want is to be happy; to be secure and comfortable; to be loved and loving and, above all, to know that you are always safe. These qualities are the natural states of EMPTINESS.

Why is fear, guilt, and control so prevalent in this world?

Our natural state is Emptiness, which means innocence, love, peace, happiness and just BEING. However, if as a child we are deprived of our natural state by feeling unloved, unwanted and therefore unhappy, we seek power as a substitute. Power is the need for control, in other words, the need and craving to get your own way regardless of others.

If I am innocent by nature, how can I prevent others from manipulating me?

If you are truly innocent, then the need to prevent others from manipulating you is redundant. Your innocence means that you see only goodness and so, through the law of attraction, you are led to people whom you can trust. Life always takes care of us when we are EMPTY of control, fear, and guilt.

The *Course* says, "you need do nothing." So how can that bring results I want?

When you allow yourself to be empty, then you are automatically attracted to that which is good in your life. Why? Life is good.

Take the body as an example. Did you know that the body is constantly healing itself? However, when we digress and ignore the body's need for good thoughts and food, it gives us warnings by giving us uncomfortable symptoms. However, instead of listening to the symptoms as lessons we need to listen and learn from, we try to suppress them by taking drugs to get rid of the symptoms and, that's how we destroy life's gift to us. We need to listen to the body.

When we allow EMPTINESS to be our daily life, then LISTENING awakens in us. We become more alert in the NOW, and we are triggered by LOVE to do what we are meant to do.

How can we get rid of guilt, control, and fear in order to be empty?

Emptiness is your natural state when you allow yourself to "be."

The world teaches us that if we relax then nothing is done. This appears to be true because our LOVE has not been awakened.

Love is also our natural state. When love is missing, then the need to control comes into play, and we are in mischief. However, mischief brings suffering and misery and thus, by listening to what we are doing to ourselves restores our listening.

What do you mean by listening?
Listening is like watching or tuning in. You become still and check your feelings at this moment. If there is stress, you'll immediately know that you're out of alignment with your thinking and feeling. In this case become still. Be aware that you are not feeling good and turn to the emptiness known as Holy Spirit and give this lack of goodness to the Holy Spirit to take care of it. It is as simple as that.

That's a new twist. Is Emptiness the Holy Spirit then?
Yes, of course. The word Holy means whole, complete, nothing to be added. The word Spirit means the emptiness, the perfection of "Being" such as pure thought, pure feeling, and pure awareness.

Purity is nature's way of being. Organic food simply means natural food before human manipulation destroyed it by GMO, preservatives, and other poisons.

If the Holy Spirit is our natural state of Being, then why pray to it?
Prayer is the natural communication of the soul to itself since everything is one consciousness. If you are not aligned with your nature, then you pray to be aligned again.

I still find it hard to do nothing and be nothing?
This question is common because there's always the thought that we do things instead of the Holy Spirit through us. In this case let me quote the *Course*: "Save time for me by only one preparation and practice doing nothing else, 'I need do nothing.' This is a

statement of allegiance, a truly undivided loyalty. Believe it for just one instant, and you will accomplish more than given to a century of contemplation or struggle against temptation."

Why do we rely on our ego and create so much suffering?
The average human being is so removed from knowing oneself that he or she feels alone. We are one-BEing in the entire Universe. We are part of each other. In this unity, we come to know ourselves as love. When the human and the being become one, then loneliness is no longer experienced and one moments' prayer or meditation will "bring" the connection. It is through this oneness that all answers come to us. They do not come through words but through feeling.

How does feeling bring an answer?
The answer will come as a feeling where questions become redundant. This redundancy is itself the answer. *There is nothing happening in your world except that which is expressive and reflective of your thinking process at any given moment.*

So how do we give up trying with our limited thinking to do everything?
We need to involve body-awareness.

Involving Body-Awareness

The *Course* says about the body, "The ego's temple thus becomes the temple of the Holy Spirit, where devotion to him replaces devotion to the ego. In this sense, the body does BECOME a temple to God because his voice abides in it by directing the use to which it is put."

The above quote is very significant in maintaining optimum health. What happens to most people is that the moment something goes wrong with the body and feels pain or discomfort, we go to the doctor and are given drugs to suppress this pain or discomfort. This is the ego's way which makes our body much worse by not listening to it. By listening to the body's act or discomfort, we come to know how we are misaligned from love (not eating proper nutritious organic food, not drinking enough pure water, or indulging in pleasure food.) Taking good care of the body is simply eating natural food such as organic vegetables and fruit.

Most often diseases and discomforts emerge from stress—fear, anxiety, depression, guilt, and anger are causes of physical dis-ease.

When we identify with the body as "who" we are, we separate from our Spirit-essence, which is our emptiness and so cause automatic stress. Stress is caused by often feeling overwhelmed by how many things we have to do instead of allowing them to happen through us.

Here are some facts about the body:

- The body may age over the years but never need to grow old.
- The body repairs itself. It's been built to heal itself. All we need do is align with love.
- Our higher Self (Holy Spirit) gives us messages on how to take care of the body and heal. It guides us through what we love to do.
- When we feel pain, we usually try to take the pain away by taking a pain pill. Don't!
- The body talks to us through discomfort, fatigue, weakness and pain. If we don't listen and medicate it, then things worsen and become serious. You can't ignore the body's signals.

- By getting in touch with the chakras, you get to know what's ailing you. For example, the Manipuri chakra (stomach) is the power center. Control and anger can cause many problems there. The heart chakra is love, disappointments, rejection, anger, deep hurt, etc., affecting the heart.
- Keep healthy by following natural means. Listen to Nature.

In the classic book, *Perfect Health*, channeled by the world-famous Elwood Babbit, he said, "We have known people under bondage to such belief for years to be internally released from it and awakened from it by saying the following:

"I am Spirit through and through, and no material thing I contact can have any effect on me to produce disagreement or pain. I am given dominion over everything, and nothing can make me afraid."

In the book, *Wherever You Go There You Are*, it says: "Non-doing has nothing to do with being indolent or passive. Quite the contrary. It takes courage and energy to cultivate non-doing, both in stillness and in activity. Nor is it easy to make a special time for non-doing and to keep at it in the face of everything in our lives which needs to be done."

Osho said, "We fear nothingness. We try to keep busy in order not to contemplate it. And, when we do avoid it or fear it, the nothing-ness becomes a heart-wrenching emptiness, loneliness, and inner desperation. So, we try to have many things to do, keep busy and involved and lose touch with our feelings. We try to get high to get away from this inner emptiness. We try drugs, alcohol, parties and many such activities.

The emptiness you feared is not Emptiness. It was just a wrong interpretation of the conditioned ego mind. True nothingness is not nothingness but FULLNESS!"

The Second GROUND-BREAKING Unknown *Fact of* Reality

The Fear of Emptiness

Humankind is beset with fears—fear of old age, fear of death, fear of illness and pain, fear of failure, fear of others, fear of oneself, self-consciousness, uneasiness, discomfort, doubts, uncertainties, insecurities and continual stress in simply living life.

Where did all these come from? Listen carefully . . .

There is only one source from which all these fears have come from—one single fear. It is the greatest fear known to humankind. It is the fear of emptiness, of being no more!

The *Course* says: "Man's mind can be possessed by illusions, but his Spirit is eternally free. If a mind perceives without love, it perceives an empty shell and is unaware of the Spirit within it. But the atonement (oneness) restores the Soul to its proper place. The mind that serves the Spirit is invulnerable."

Oneness or Atonement means being one with the moment without being scattered. It is the ability to restore to the truth of the moment and to be one with it. This moment is the witness, the observer, the detached looker at what-is. So, if one observes without love, with awareness, then there is this fear of emptiness. On the other hand, when one starts observing with focus, with the desire to experience the truth, then he will realize that the emptiness he feared so desperately was the eternal Spirit of Truth itself! This is the paradox—the moment you allow yourself to feel the emptiness, then viola, you experience fullness!

Try it now. Become very still and do some slow deep stomach breathing. Shed everything that you think you are such as past, identity, name, title, expectations, fears, beliefs, etc. Throw them all out until you feel empty. Then allow this emptiness without expecting a result. See what happens . . .

You will feel fullness, freedom, fearlessness, and completeness.

Remember in this SECOND UNKNOWN FACT OF REALITY that it's this fear that drives people to commit suicide, to go insane and driven to desperation—the fear of emptiness. Strange how we fear the very liberation; we fear the very salvation; we fear the unconditional love we crave so much unconsciously. What if you realized this right now?

To realize his truth is so blessed that you won't stop laughing in an utter explosion of awakening. We fear the very thing we want most. After all, what's the unconditional love that many NDEs experience? Isn't it this very emptiness that suddenly becomes the Light of Heaven. Repeating, to realize the emptiness you feared so desperately was, and is, the eternal Spirit of Truth!

What generally happens is this: whenever we are buffeted by life's down spiral, we look for answers from others which rarely help. When we look within, we find emptiness and get depressed, frightened and often feel like drowning into an abyss. This is the fear we avoid at all costs. We start keeping active mentally to avoid looking into this emptiness. It's this very activity of mind that compounds the fears. We can't escape the truth. Our attempts to escape create anxieties and panic attacks. It becomes a vicious circle. This is the insanity of this one great fear—the fear of emptiness.

It seems that the only time we look at emptiness is whenever we are unhappy. And so, we perceive an empty shell like the *Course* said. If on the other hand, we allowed ourselves to consciously and deliberately look into this emptiness, when we are relaxed and happy, we would find only Silence. It's this Silence of Spirit, which unbeknown to us, is the inner answer to all questions.

Please read again the underlined statements above and FEEL in your heart what it's truly saying. This is your liberation; your freedom; your truth.

A fear is never real. Only imagination makes it seem so.

Remember the four letters of fear. F.E.A.R. They spell, False Evidence Appearing Real!

Fear is a separation you are creating from yourself, and that's how all insanity, craziness, desperation and psychological attacks are created.

One day, many years ago, I was waiting in a long line of people wanting to Photostat some papers at the library.

One woman behind me panicked, "I feel suffocated!" she exclaimed and ran outside for some air. She felt confined and panicked. When she was outside, she felt better temporarily. However, she was running away from herself but didn't know it.

When we demand space from people, we are asking for the space we don't give ourselves. People are us. We are all people. We think it's happening out there, but it's all in here. It's a fear of emptiness. To repeat, when we fear emptiness, we suffer suffocation, loneliness, smallness, etc. In a crowded situation, you feel lost, confined, restricted, stifled as if you can't breathe. The ego feels unprotected, feels as if its drowning and so it runs away. Every time it runs away it reinforces its fear. It is this need to run away that creates the panic.

How do you heal this?

The moment you start feeling as if you want to run away, pause. Take a deep breath from the stomach a few times and then smile saying inwardly, "This awareness has made me stronger."

When we face the fearful emptiness, we also create the positive and powerful emptiness of Spirit Love. It's this courage that gives us self-love.

Remember that emptiness feels horrible to the ego and yet feels freedom and love to the Spirit Being. Emptiness, when faced, is Fullness.

The image of emptiness is either liberating to the faithful in heart or petrifying to the faint at heart. How we view emptiness is what makes the difference between weakness and strength.

The average human finds emptiness terrible and lonely, and it lingers like a shadow. The AWARE human, on the other hand, sees emptiness as pure being filled with love, courage, fullness and enchantment.

Here are some examples (thinking), "I'm going to lose my lover and then feel alone."

Why do we fear being alone? Isn't it the fear of emptiness?

Another form of this fear is, "I feel threatened by people's criticism and get angry easily or upset."

Why is that? It's the fear of emptiness because you want to believe you are this or that, somehow afraid that you might be empty and so protect an image that doesn't exist. It's but an image.

The Founder of Psycho-Synthesis Assagioli wrote, "We spend 95% of our energy protecting, defending and maintaining our self-image when all it is, is but an image."

I have some issues I want to deal with, and they are not fears but daily discomforts.

Another example is, "He/She left me and I want closure." This is another game of the ego propelled by the denial of the fear of emptiness. All discomforts, all issues are fears. All fears stem from the fear of emptiness.

A fear is a protection of your ego. Getting rid of a fear is frightening to the ego because it would mean leaving yourself vulnerable and thus feeling empty. This is the reason fears are repeated over and over again. Unconsciously, we really don't want to get rid of them. So, we pretend by going to a therapist. If one doesn't work, we go to another one. But the fears don't go away because there is no such fear as we think. Real Emptiness is egolessness which means we have found our true Self of love, joy, peace and fullness of Being.

Here s a great truth I ignored for most of my life working as a therapist. Therapy doesn't work because it's based on the premise that you're an ego. What works is awareness of your emptiness. This is why I changed the practice of hypnotherapy into "SuperSentience."

SuperSentience works on the same principle as hypnotherapy, but its focus is on Super-Sentience which means awareness of awareness as one's true nature. The Presence, witness, watcher is looking at looking.

Ego is Attachment to Surface Values

There is nothing more frightening, more desperate, more chilling than emptiness perceived with attachment. To be attached seeking answers feels like we are falling into an abyss, a meaningless existence. Why is it like this?

Emptiness is our true nature. Attachment to the false ego is not our true nature but simply a hypnotized or conditioned illusion. For example, we identify with our body without recognizing that the body was created from Spirit Essence or nothingness (emptiness).

The ego, which is strong identification with the body, is just an image. Although psychologists encourage a positive self-image, it's still an image and not truth. Thus, attachment to the personality, as opposed to your true nature, creates an imbalance. Psychology teaches you how to cope but not to transcend.

The Two Kinds of Emptiness

As a teen, I always felt lonely despite having lots of friends. I was always an outsider looking in. I experienced a chilling emptiness that often embraced the idea of suicide. This emptiness could never be filled because it identified with my body as "me," separate from others. Later, when I awakened somewhat from Bhagavan's teachings, I realized that my emptiness was based on comparison and separation and, that's when I "saw" clearly that true emptiness was the Spirit of Oneness where separation was impossible. The emptiness I feared was an abyss from which I could fall into and disappear forever, whereas true Emptiness was the fullness of Being, Oneness and Source itself known as Holy Spirit. This is the Source of everything that appeared as form and objective.

The Western movie, *Tombstone,* depicted Ringo as a deranged killer who enjoyed torturing people. Wyatt Earp was at the bedside of the dying Doc Holliday. Wyatt asked Doc, "What makes a man like Ringo do what he does?" And Doc replied, "Ringo has a great empty hole in the middle of him which he is trying to get rid of, and he can never do enough killing, enough raping, enough stealing and torturing to fill it."

What is that empty hole we are all trying to fill and never succeed?

What is that feeling as if something is missing?

What is that feeling of never being good enough?

Why does it plague humanity?

And yet, most people feel this inner discomfort and don't even know they have it. Most people are not in touch with their feelings. Ask yourself this, "Am I happy or living another Ingmar Bergman movie?"

Most people have lived in misery so long they actually believe it's life itself. This is the sleep most everyone is in. Even when children are playing, laughing and enjoying themselves, we say, "Let them enjoy it while they can for soon innocence is lost, and they will find out life is hard and miserable."

I remember watching a movie where the son was holding

his dying father's hand. The father says, "Son, life is a bitch. You work hard, grow old, and then you die." In a way, he was right because that is the life of the unawakened soul.

All Fear is Fear of Emptiness

All fear is fear of emptiness as if losing something and feeling less. To recognize this fact is a great step in awareness growth. The purpose of this chapter is to bring this awareness to you, for this awareness alone can create a tremendous leap in consciousness expansion.

The issues we take to a therapist are nothing more than fear of emptiness. Once this fact is confronted, then permanent healing is possible.

Here is another fact. All fear of emptiness is an illusion. Illusion cannot be overcome; it cannot even be healed unless seen to be an illusion.

Once it's seen through and through, then it automatically disappears as if it never existed. This is the paradox of healing such fear. We see its illusion clearly and realize it was all unconscious imagination made real.

Here are some real examples: (The following are actual cases I treated in hypnotherapy.)

<u>Fear of Abandonment</u> – She carried it in the pit of her stomach as a feeling of being left all alone. She remembered as a two-year-old being left alone and terrified in her playpen. When she realized it was continual fear of emptiness, being alone, abandoned, she saw through it.

<u>Feeling Unworthy</u> – He was often depressed. He had a big knot in his stomach. His early life included some horrendous parental violence, leaving a legacy of low self-worth. He used to say, "I

feel unworthy as if I'm nothing." He was afraid of the emptiness that was the very undiscovered love in him. Once he recognized this, he was released.

Being Intimidated at Work – She had a rage-filled, abusive supervisor. The supervisor stood over her and continually pointed out the errors. She was blamed for everything. She believed, "If I expressed my power, I'd be killed." Fear of death is fear of emptiness, feeling finished as if no more.

She regained her confidence and love of herself when she recognized that fear of emptiness was fear of herself. After recognizing that, she was able to look straight into her supervisor's eyes and remain strong. The abuse stopped.

The Feeling of Loneliness – He felt an abiding sense of loneliness. He was often left in his high chair and completely ignored. No one seemed to know he was there. He believed he was always alone, separate, empty. When he got in touch with his emptiness, he became a new man.

Fear of the Past – Everyone has abused her in her family. As a girl, she was raped and beaten by her father. Her past was too painful to recall. She believed that if she faced her past, it would swallow her up. Thus, she was in constant emotional pain. When it was made plain to her that her fear was fear of her own emptiness, the memories of her past stopped interfering with her life.

Sexual Problem – He can't help thinking about sex most of the time and yet when he performs loses his erection. He remembered his father standing over him and judging him. He felt he was constantly being judged. Feeling judged comes from the inner emptiness as if something is missing. When he looked into it, he discovered fear of his own inner love.

Prosperity Problem – She never had enough money although competent and able. She believed in a small voice inside her that said, "Nothing can come to any good." She believed she was not good enough. Feeling not good enough is fear of emptiness. It's the fear of something missing.

Powerlessness in Relationship – He was married to someone outspoken and verbally abusive. He felt like a doormat. He believed he had no power. He felt empty and powerless until he recognized the emptiness he feared was love itself.

Feeling Rage – She felt betrayed by her mentor. In her youth, her father betrayed her. This repeated because she believed in her inability to be loved for herself. The feeling of not trusting is a result of inner emptiness suspecting that others are just as empty and not trustworthy. When she discovered that she could trust her own emptiness, she also awoke to her own love.

Love and Fear of Emptiness

There are only two emotions—love or fear! All that is positive and good is love. It's our true nature, and that's why we always want to feel good.

Fear, on the other hand, is when love is not experienced fully in our heart, and so we doubt our feelings. Fear which is false evidence appearing real is made up of uncertainty, doubt, skepticism, insecurity, and so on. Fear is a subtle feeling of having lost something or about to lose something. It's a sense that something is missing or incomplete, and thus it's emptiness of a negative nature. When we REALIZE our true nature as pure being, empty of ego, then we discover inner silence, tranquility, peace, love and joy. The different states of emptiness make the difference between love and fear. Great Masters always knew that they were empty and so their presence was immediately felt as magnetic and powerful. Feeling initially empty is a self-conscious stage. When you realize that you don't need courses or learning to acquire peace, love, joy and fulfillment, then you discover your own unique Emptiness which is also Fullness.

There are three stages of emptiness:

1. The first stage is the ME stage: This is the self-conscious stage where it looks like there's so much to learn. In this stage, you believe you are your body. You feel separate and also insecure about who you are. This is Fear of emptiness.
2. This second stage is the Self-Aware stage which means that you are finally becoming aware of how we are all the same. You are aware of how and what you think and so are stronger in your mind. This is the seeking, and also, the beginning of the awakening stage. You still feel negative emptiness.
3. This third stage is the I AM stage and totally loves Emptiness. You are empty from the mind's conditioning. Emptiness here means Holy Spirit; Wholeness; Oneness; fullness and integration of Self. Here you are in love with the Light of unconditional love. Fear is the undiscovered love in us, so, when we have had no love than we are controlled by fear, guilt, and need for power.

Why Does Fear Feed on Itself?

Fear feeds itself simply because we are afraid of it and so it gathers momentum. It is a vicious circle. Fear engenders more fear until we are afraid of fear itself. For example, I would say to someone, "It's okay. I will be here with you, just go into the fear and see its emptiness."

The response is often, "But I'm afraid of the fear." Even when we recognize we are afraid, we become afraid of being afraid. We become more afraid that we will never get rid of this fear. This is the vicious circle of fear and why people become emotionally unbalanced.

There's only one way to rise above the fear. It is to see the Truth. The truth is that the fear of emptiness is the love we unconsciously seek.

So, why are we so afraid of love when it's all we really want? The answer is simple. Pure love is the emptiness, and that would mean egolessness. Ego known as the "me" is so self-preoccupied and identified that it is fully convinced it is "who I am." Therefore, emptiness of me feels like death until we actually do it and find that we are now in love—truly and fully in love like all awakened human beings are.

Always remain aware that emptiness of ego conditioning is the fullness of joy.

The ego's greatest fear is being without an ego. Ego is the belief that it's our identity, and yet in truth, our identity is I AM which is the Light of us. The ego's function is non-stop seeking for answers and results, which never happens. This is why ego is always seeking love with attachment that can't last. And since ego is possessive it's often jealous, restless and afraid of loss. Do you know what happens when the ego finds the love it wants?

It sabotages it! The ego has nothing to give because it can't love.

You are the Presence of LOVE!

Ask yourself right now, "Who am I?" and no matter how sincere and honest you attempt this question, you will find Emptiness. You can't be the body just because you occupy it. You can't be your name just because you own it. You can't be the past just because you have lived it. It lives in memory only. You can't be your education and training because you've experienced these things, also.

So, who are you really?

Your answer doesn't depend upon what you own but what you are. So, what are you right now? Really feel it.

You are the Emptiness of Pure Awareness. You "just know" that you simply are this moment's presence. This Presence, which is the real YOU right now is love itself. Feel it at this moment's Silence how you know you "just-are!" This knowing is your birthright, your truth, your Being and your Emptiness that is ever FULL!

Are you now closer to understanding who you are?

A Course in Miracles states in lesson #48, "In truth, there is absolutely nothing to fear. It is very easy to recognize this. But it's very difficult for those who want illusions to be real."

Of course, the word "illusions" refers to all that which comes and goes and has no permanent expression or reality. However, the Presence was never born and never dies and never changes. Can you see the glory of this great Truth? We keep evolving in Presence experiencing greater and greater glories that totally blow the mind away.

In the book, *I Come as a Brother*; it states, "Fear is that dark and difficult side of the human movement towards freedom and love that we choose to call fear. It's really a lack of understanding. In truth, there is nothing to fear."

Why does fear of emptiness create complications?

Fear of emptiness makes you feel incomplete, and so one develops a great desire to learn. In this desire comes all kinds of psychological studies. i.e. How to improve relationships; how to be a better person; how to understand the brain; how to be smarter and so on and on endlessly. There are literally millions of courses to take. Yet, if you stop learning and DISCOVER WHO YOU ARE you will reach the highest success in life called fulfillment.

You don't need to learn anything. All you need is to discover yourself!

Once you discover the truth of your Being what else is there?

Fulfillment in life does not happen through learning and improvement but through DISCOVERY!

I know that this sounds contradictory to our social understanding. It's very revolutionary but, yet it's the Truth. It doesn't mean you don't learn how to use your phone or computer etc. It means simply that learning information doesn't make you a better human being. You can't add one iota to you by learning information but only by discovering your true essential and eternal nature. Then everything simply comes to you by itself after discovery.

Prior to Self-discovery is the need and seeking of information believing that through information we awaken. Millions of spiritual books are sold annually, and needy people devour them only to remain the same after reading. Why? Reading, if not followed by Self-Discovery becomes just another accumulation to the mind and therefore more mental activity.

People don't improve through learning more information. They simply become more active mentally and emotionally. Whereas, Self-discovery brings peace, harmony, patience, love and trust.

What makes people difficult & controlling?

This is an interesting question which is seldom asked. People become difficult and controlling when they do not know themselves and so are still gripped by fear of emptiness.

And, here's the solution: Self-discovery!

Let's cover this in more detail . . .

Imagine a mother who's separated from her husband and has grown married children and lives alone. Chances are, if not spiritually awakened (which means she hasn't discovered herself) lives in constant unconscious fear of being abandoned by her children. Thus, she becomes controlling to have some hold. Otherwise she'll feel empty and lost.

Now, what if she got in touch with her emptiness and found it to be love? Remember that unawakened emptiness is misery and loneliness, but awakened emptiness is unconditional love. What are the chances of such a person doing that? Not likely! This is the game and strategy of the ego to keep itself in control and thus live in continual fear.

Here is an important point to remember: fear of emptiness becomes the need to control either the environment or people close to you.

Seven Controlling Ploys

There are seven manipulating ploys which controllers use on others:

1. Guilt: This is used to hurt or control others. "How can you do this to me?' "After all, I have done for you?" "How can you do this to your mother?"
2. Anger: This is especially effective against those unnerved by openly aggressive behavior.

3. Criticism: The manipulator finds something wrong with the other person's thinking or behavior and uses criticism to upset his mental balance and make him feel insecure.
4. Obligation: This is often introduced in the form of an unspoken agreement. In other words, "If I do this for you, you'll have to do this for me."
5. Withholding: Primarily used in close relationships. Silent treatment or withholding sexual love.
6. Helplessness: The manipulator claims that he can't do what he needs to do unless you do what he wants you to do.
7. Questioning: The manipulator asks questions to which he already knows the answers, usually to make the other person admit that they were wrong or in error.

It All Depends Upon How We See Emptiness

Emptiness is truth because we are pure eternal and infinite Spirit appearing to own a body and conditioned time and space. Emptiness has no ego to control, manipulate or to have hate, fear or guilt. Emptiness is like the innocent child who looks without control with love. Emptiness is like the puppy who loves because he is love. Emptiness is Spirit and the God in us. Emptiness is like the clear blue sky ever shining and alive. It is our very being, our very energy, and life force. Emptiness is the magnetic yet innocent force of the awakened Master. However, we have so identified with name and form that we believe there is nothing else. And, because we have so identified with name and form, we believe that emptiness is a shallow grave or abyss and we fear it. However again, it's this very fear of emptiness, once understood, that can help us awaken to the truth.

We hardly ever inquire into our true nature and, instead,

we try to fill our emptiness with information to appear as if we know the truth, and thus create belief systems. If we take a look at the Internet, we find millions of courses of information are offered plus so many expensive courses on behavior, relationship, mastery and improvement and yet hardly a word about DISCOVERY OF WHO AND WHAT WE ARE!

This is repeated through this book to bring a remembrance of what is important—the discovery of YOU right now even as you read this.

Do the following: place two pointing fingers against each other with only one inch apart. Keep looking at that space in between them until you see the energy that emanates from them. The moment you see this energy, however subtle, look out and around you and see how everything is that energy (that empty energy).

Seeing the energy of emptiness everywhere is a great start towards self-discovery. Everything is energy and, this energy became both solid matter and living things. This is the source of emptiness, and although initially it's felt as heaviness and loneliness, it turns out to be, by awakening to its truth, a Lightness, and Joy.

Emptiness is a presence and it can't be avoided. Wherever you are there you are. You can never escape yourself. This is why we need to wake up from our nightmare and discover truth. To repeat, Truth is Emptiness that initially feels like a hollow abyss, but upon seeing it truly, it becomes as the fullness of love and joy and glory.

What is Your Goal in Life?

When we expend our energy trying to become successful, rich, famous or simply to be special somebody to be noticed, we never stop to ask why we need to do that. It is all an escape from emptiness, which is fear itself. Repeating never to be forgotten (and the value of this book), to discover the beauty of your Emptiness is to automatically become fullness. Emptiness is the love we seek in people and objects. When we don't realize this, it becomes fear of emptiness. Fear of emptiness is fear of love. Fear of love is called emotional pain which psychologists have given various names such as anxiety attacks, paranoia, borderline, etc.

Now we know why relationships are mostly co-dependent and that's very painful. It's what the *Course* calls "special relationships" to give ourselves the love we never gave ourselves.

Our daily life is filled with escapes and confronting our emptiness. The ego is very devious and will find things to keep you occupied so that you find excuses NOT to LOOK at the things you fear.

The average career-minded person escapes through workaholism.

The housewife escapes through so much work to do, busy with the children and shopping.

The person without work starts practicing spirituality, and that forms another escape.

What does emptiness feel like without spiritual awakening?

- feel itchy
- restless
- bored
- not knowing what to do
- feel incomplete
- feel something is missing
- feel as if you're not good enough
- moody
- changeable
- feels like a pebble in your shoe

- like an itch you can't scratch
- don't know what you want
- fear of death

. . . and a few others.

The Truth is this: awakening is the simplest thing there is.

All it entails is a moment of LOOKING at your emptiness without judgment and going into its "empty" state despite the fear.

This willingness to confront your emptiness will be to do the following: It will give us the courage to confront our fear of death and in turn, will give you so much more . . .

1. It will bring total clarity of how things really are.
2. Knowledge of our deathlessness; a certainty that comes from the heart.
3. It will transcend all fears.
4. It will bring an innocent joy and peace and inner richness that the egoic mind can't conceive.
5. It will awaken a new love we never knew existed.
6. We see clearly how our true nature is unconditional love and supreme joy.

The *Course* says, "When you learn to make me manifest, you will never see death. For you would have looked upon the deathless in yourself, and you will only see the eternal as you look out upon a world that cannot die." (T.217)

In the teacher's manual page 63, it says, "Death is the central dream from which all illusions stem."

Why call it emptiness?

Science has taught us life is made up of particles and waves. They are interchangeable but co-exist. They are interrelated and interdependent.

A particle lives in time and space. A wave lives beyond time and space.

Therefore, a wave is a movement of emptiness such as audio waves, cellular phone waves, radio waves, Skype video/audio waves, etc., which are invisible to the naked eye but make us feel love. Thus, a wave is a movement of emptiness. Emptiness is pure nothingness, energy, stillness. When energy moves, it creates waves. For example, we hear the radio through radio waves and talk on our cell phones through the same audio waves. Technology is made up of waves and particles.

Our body is a particle made up of trillions of cells, but we live through the wave that we are. Now, through unawareness, we have separated the particle from the wave, and that has become our biggest emotional pain. We have identified with the particle and forgot that it was the wave that made the particle possible. We cannot separate emptiness from the wave, or the wave from the particle. They are interrelated, interdependent and interconnected. Therefore, it is ALL EMPTINESS.

Emptiness is like death to us. We believe that death is the end of things, which is absurd since emptiness has no beginning nor end. It is beyond time and space and when the particle appears, then so too does the semblance of time and space from the motion of particles. For example, the earth's rotation around the sun creates the minutes, hours, days, weeks, months and seasons but all it is is a movement of the earth around the sun. Just as unawareness brings emptiness of feeling, depression, and fear, so does the awakening and understanding of emptiness brings freedom, liberation, love and great joy beyond the mind. It's the mind and brain that bring limited understanding, believe it or not. I didn't know that truth until I had the Light experience in the hospital. I learned more in a few minutes than all my years before.

Why does death take place?

First of all, there is only NOW which is deathless. NOW itself, beyond time, doesn't know death. However, what we call death is the end of the particle that separates from the wave. The particle shifts into another expression whereas the wave remains intact as YOU with all the memory, choices, and the greatest love you have ever experienced. Yet, fear, guilt, and negativity cannot exist because they are only created by time and space.

The British Yogi Master, Richard Hittleman, was asked, "If you know you are dying, what would you attempt to envision at the moment of death?"

He answered, "Find out if you are 'alive' before you concern yourself with death."

They didn't understand, and so he continued, "You have identified yourself with a body. You know that the body dies and so you think that you die also. But your true nature, Self, is not born and cannot die. Recognize your true nature for it JUST IS!"

When you begin to understand the nature of energy, you will discover what is called "dead" or "alive" are simply viewpoints.

Misunderstood emptiness is death.

Awakened emptiness is aliveness!

Are we really afraid of death or the thought of it?

What frightens us is the idea of death because it represents leaving behind what is known and heading towards the unknown. The particle is the known, and the wave is the unknown. If we came to know the wave, then fear would be eliminated.

Next time you are afraid and have the willingness to expand your awareness of truth, do two things:

1. Look into the fear and see how it is fear of emptiness.

2. Look into that emptiness through allowing and accepting that emptiness, and you will discover silence, which is the Spirit of Oneness.

Awakened Emptiness is the greatest beauty of Life.

It is the only true love, the only truth we have. Fear is trying to get rid of this inner beauty, innocence, and love. However, it is all happening unconsciously. This is the great paradox of truth, the great confusion of the ego and the resulting frustration and insanity.

Summarizing Fear of Love (Emptiness)

Love is the truth of our being. It's eternal and never changing. It's all we are and ever shall be. The idea that you are a personal human being apart from others is the biggest lie we have ever known. It's this lie that the greatest teachings have referred to as the original sin.

The initial stages of consciousness evolution start out as the feeling of separation. This belief in separation is known as fear. The fear is not of separation but of love. It is the fear of love that starts the suffering. The question might arise, "Why should we fear love when it's who we are?" Because we believe we are separate, and therefore our heart knowing our oneness reaches out for this love expression. In reaching out it feels like a need for love, a need to be loved by another. This need becomes neediness and therefore exhibits itself as loneliness, anxiety, feeling of limitation, lack, sense of incompleteness and starts us striving to complete ourselves through effort. We try to improve, grow and adjust, progress, and it's all part of the play of consciousness. However, in our reason for love, we never attempt to love ourselves. The reason is clear.

We have believed we are separate and therefore feel a lack

and reach out to be loved by another to feel completion. The only way we can relate to love initially is through having someone love us. The trick is this: the ego that seeks love can't love because it's the belief of separation, in limitation and lack. Do you see now why we fear love when, at the same time, seek it? It's this "play" of hide and seek which is emotional suffering.

The Third GROUND-BREAKING Unknown *Fact of* Reality

The Wonder of Unconditional Love

Here is the one Truth that binds all humanity as One—unconditional love, It's the Secret of Life on Earth.

The first ground-breaking fact was, and is, emptiness and how it all plays—the drama, games, fears and loves of humanity. Emptiness is as frightening initially to the unawakened as it's the most glorious experience of inner Heaven (Home).

To make it all simple: all fears, insecurities, inadequacies, discomforts and emotional suffering stem from the feeling of emptiness. Emptiness can be gut-wrenching suffering. It continues to be suffering until we see that IT, ITSELF is the key to our Home.

When we can look at our emptiness and fully see its miracle as our Kingdom of Heaven on earth, then we come Home.

What is unconditional Love, but the greatest of the greatest! It awakens when we clearly see that Emptiness is itself unconditional love.

Strange how suffering makes us seek love in relationships, in love-stories, in romance, in songs, in our dreams. Yet, we don't see how, in all of this, we are seeking who we are—our true essential nature.

Did you ever get away from the city to find the peace and tranquility of Nature, and then find it on a mountain, in a forest, near the ocean, even in an object of Nature?

One Satsang, I was talking about the beauty of Nature and its silence. A woman who was visibly stressed told me that she was going away to the mountains to commune with Nature. I could see from her eyes that she truly meant it. I saw her after a few months, and she was a completely changed woman. I asked her what she experienced, and it was something so simple that brought tears to my eyes. She said, "After a month by myself in the woods and I had finished my novel, I was ready to head for home. Then on my way home in the city, I saw in the cement a crack. And in that crack, I witnessed a flower forcing its way to the surface. At that moment as I looked in awe and wonder, I was filled with the wonder of unconditional love. Even in the most horrendous suffering the love we are reaches out to teach us."

Even in the greatest suffering from emptiness, we can LOOK at that emptiness and find that, in itself, emptiness is, itself, the Silence and stillness of unconditional love. Our true Home.

I remember reading about a Satsang teacher (Ananda Kranti) who woke up in a Japanese prison cell. They kept huddled together without making a sound or move. If they made the slightest move or sound, they were beaten. One day this young woman keeping still unable to move lest she got beaten suddenly realized such stillness and emptiness that even her mind stopped thinking. Suddenly she felt as if she was drowning in this emptiness and she let go, allowing herself to drown into this emptiness. Then, from nowhere, emptiness became the fullness and she clearly saw that it was all a game and started laughing. Her laughter enraged the guards as they beat her, but nothing mattered. She was suddenly free in her joy of full emptiness that reached its epitome of grace. They released her thinking she went crazy. Now she is a wonderful Satsang teacher.

Just as emptiness is a gut-wrenching fear, yet in it is carried the seed of fullness when surrendered and fully allowed. The *Course* calls this "allowing" forgiveness itself. Forgiveness is not something we "do" but simply allow to happen as we watch it.

The Miracle of LOOKING

We have learned a great deal up to this point. We have learned how simple everything is such as the wave and the particle. We see the particle but do not see the wave. The wave, which makes everything possible, is emptiness itself, non-material, invisible, unseen, yet it's everywhere. If we have a sophisticated radio, we can tune in to Germany, Australia, and other remote places if they are sending radio signals. We can close windows and yet these wave signals are reached, just as we use our cell phone or Skype on the computer from long distances. Waves defy time and space to reach us as sound waves, video waves, radio waves, etc. How and why? Again, because waves defy time and space and therefore they are everywhere at the same time.

The miracle of technology is making our world smaller and reachable. It's making us realize that emptiness is the fullness of Being. The more we grow, the more we reach each other. The more we reach other, we see that we have no enemies because we are all the same. War creates enemies because war is the unawareness of love and so creates separation and suffering. War tries to control emptiness by trying to create more and more. Whereas, we learn that war only brings misery and there are no victors. Eventually, we will discover that war cannot defeat emptiness by bringing more and more. Emptiness can only be won by seeing it for the first time as it actually IS!

Allowing Emptiness as Your Biggest Lesson

How do you allow emptiness?

By looking into it! Start by acknowledging that there is emptiness being experienced as fear, restlessness, seeking, striving, overloaded mental activity and so on. Then, accept this overload as your suffering. The moment you allow it by not being concerned, it reaches a stillness, a quietness of being. You simply relax into it like saying, "So what?" Thus, this emptiness becomes stillness. In stillness, breathe slowly deeply watching your whole body relax into it without struggling against it.

Now, this emptiness starts shifting into deeper Emptiness such as tranquility, quiet mind, peace. Soon joy will begin to flower. This is the beginning of love enhancement. This is the start of awakening love.

Love is What It's All About

Love is not developed but awakened from its dormant state. Love is the peaceful, quiet but fully alive energy of Being.

Love is openness and innocence of heart. Ask yourself, "What qualities do you seek in people?" and it's always a form of emptiness (Presence) such as openness, sincerity, realness, innocence with intelligence, clarity, inner beauty, sweetness and a form of grace. These are all qualities that emerge from emptiness of conditioned mind. How are these qualities empty—empty from guile, from pretension, from manipulation, from control, from moodiness and majorly empty from selfishness and maliciousness?

When the mind empties itself from conditioning, the past, and isn't concerned about the future, living in the moment, it becomes empty like the child's eyes and expression.

Did you ever wonder why love is so powerful? Most songs, lyrics, poetry, stories and so on are about love. Chances are you wouldn't know why and that's normal. Love cannot be explained or fully understood, and every human being has an opinion about it until they awaken to the great fact: love is who you are, period.

Love expands in three stages:

1. First, is seeking love or seeking power. Power is the need for control because we haven't experienced love in childhood.
2. We recognize that everyone is looking for love whether in a relationship, or in appreciation, or in feeling wanted

and respected or in simply belonging. This recognition brings awakening of love.

3. This is the stage where you see everyone as yourself, the I AM! This is the full blooming of love and spiritual awakening.

Prior to the awakening of love, there is often a point of challenge known as the dark night of the soul. This happens when we fail to realize that emptiness is not a negative but a natural state of Being.

This happens at Stage 3 (see the Stages of Awakening above). Instead of accepting the emptiness as the gift of Being, it is still seen as deprivation. It's here that the dark night rears its head.

Emptiness and Fullness are One

Conceptually it seems like a contradiction to say that emptiness is fullness, yet stop thinking about it and FEEL it.

Allow yourself to feel it by doing the following: sit still and take a few slow deep breaths from the stomach counting four inhalations and six exhalations. Do this about six times.

Then having slowed down your mental activity, empty yourself by being totally here now and, throw away any thought or feeling of the past as if there's no such thing but this ever-present moment. Then see what's it like to be without a name and identity. Just be empty of everything. If you have any expectations regarding this process, then throw that out also. Just be here—EMPTY.

Keep being here and now without any thought. After a few minutes ask yourself, "Now that I have thrown everything out, what is left?"

Just be fully present as you inquire, "What is left?"

You might feel stumped by that question but just LOOK at

what is left. Aren't you still aware of being here? Who is it that is aware?

Don't answer it but let it hang there.

After a good while just LOOK at how you FEEL. Now you understand how emptiness and fullness are one.

Stages of Love Awareness

Our true nature is empty like a child's. This Emptiness is LOVE. Love is unconditional, and therefore it's not based on having some criteria or condition.

There is no limit to love just as there is no limit to Infinite Intelligence. So now the question, "How do we start to awaken our knowing of love?"

And here is the paradox of all truth. It is this: you can know to the extent that you realize you really don't know.

You see, the moment you believe you know something you have automatically limited it by your concept of thinking you know. This concept is a limitation and a stopping point because you think you know. Therefore, by thinking you know, you have reached your limit and cannot go further. How can you go further when you have reached the idea of knowing? This belief in knowing has created a stopping point and therefore also created a block to further and deeper knowing.

The more you REALIZE you don't know, the more you know of greater possibilities.

We know we are love because we are empty. This Emptiness implies that LOVE isn't an achievable thing but an expansion to include everything, including itself. Emptiness is whole and complete. It makes it complete because emptiness has no boundary line, just like timelessness and spacelessness. However, to come to this realization one needs to go through several stages of KNOWING that fully KNOWING is not logical. Intelligence is Infinite. We call it God because of its infinite nature. Now, can you know the infinite? How can you? It is infinite.

There are several stages of awareness expansion. In order to make it practical, we can say there are seven stages.

STAGE ONE: Picture the vast ocean and its surface waves. When someone looks at the ocean, all they see are the surface waves. The waves cover the ocean and make you believe that it's the whole ocean. This surface awareness, which is the average consciousness, is stage one.

STAGE TWO: This starts when we look at the ocean and recognize that there is more below the surface. We don't see what is below but know, beyond a doubt, there is more. So here, we start wanting to be more aware. This increases the urge to know more, deeper, better, improved seeing. Here is where you want to know that you know.

STAGE THREE: This stage happens when we see that our need to improve, the attainment of goals, the achievement of becoming "someone" hasn't given us fulfillment. We realize we have to go deeper and look below the surface. As we look deeper, we see the incredible depth of the ocean and get scared. Yet, we know how much we have yet to explore and experience. This depth becomes scary, and we waver wanting to grow spiritually (because we know of the depth) and yet afraid of the depth (emptiness).

This stage is the beginning of the dark night of the soul (fear of emptiness). Most people play spiritual games here pretending to know as a cover-up of that fear. Yet, even this is subconscious (beyond direct knowing of our game).

Going beyond the personal self is frightening to the conditioned self. And, it's this that causes the dark night. This is also the stage of high and low emotional feelings (fear and love). Very few ever break through this stage unless they have a guide who has been "there."

STAGE FOUR: When one has found the courage to plunge deeper into the emptiness of this ocean and looked up to see that the waves (emotions and thoughts) are surface and unreal. This being has now become detached from the "games," "stories," and pretenses that are so common in Stages 2 and 3. This, therefore, is the real beginning of awakening to one's true spiritual nature as Emptiness known as Love, Spirit, and Oneness. This fourth stage is the detachment stage.

STAGE FIVE: This is the realization that everything is just a movement of the ocean. The ocean is very still despite its waves and action. Here are unwavering peace and bliss. This is the body-awareness stage where one recognizes that all emotions are in the body because it's an expression of energy. We realize here that the body is not as real as we thought. It's the appearance of consciousness.

STAGE SIX: You find that you are no longer in the ocean—you are the ocean. You have never been anywhere or done anything. It was all an appearance of consciousness.

STAGE SEVEN: This is the fully awakened and enlightened stage. There is no longer "me" and "another." There are only us!

Love is Giving; Fear is Taking

Just as love is giving, so is fear taking. In fact, there is only emptiness. How we view it becomes our taking or giving. Giving is always grand, beautiful and expanding. Taking is always small, lonely, separate and contracted.

Picture standing outside, and it's a beautiful sunny day. However, you give your back to the sun and can only see your shadow You think you are that shadow because wherever you go, there you are. Now you feel a lack and, because of this belief of lack, you start trying to take from others in order to fill that lack. You become a beggar in life. When you turn to face the sun, you will feel its nurturing warmth, and, within that feeling become a natural giver of your light that is emanated from the sun.

In reality, there is no good or bad. There is no negative or positive. There is only taking or giving—LOVE or FEAR.

Taking always feels negative and giving always feels positive.

Here's an example. Think of all the negative feelings that are held inside and, for a moment, observe their TAKING power.

LONELINESS: "I want someone to take care of me." Yet, there's inability nor desire to care for another. If there were then loneliness would be impossible.

ANGER: "I want it this way darn it." Anger is control because there is the feeling of inner lack of control. It's trying to take what it can at that moment.

RESENTMENT: "I don't like the way you've acted." It's based on separation and, it's taking because you are not considering the other person but only the way you would like them to be.

DEPRESSION: Depression happens when the taking reaches its zenith and then there's a crash of energy. Taking zaps all energy from the soul. When enough taking has taken place, there's a general down-spiral called depression of mind, body, and soul.

PSYCHOLOGICAL FEAR: Psychological fear, which is a form of anxiety, is the feeling of losing something. "If I do that I might be embarrassed." "What if people laugh at me." "What if I fail."

The feeling of taking embodies the feeling of loss. This is where greed, selfishness, insecurity and possessiveness come from. TAKING, therefore, implies not giving of oneself for fear of loss—loss of time, loss of money, loss of recognition, loss of identity, loss of attention and so on.

In brief, all negativity is the "taking" attitude and fear of giving. Fear of giving is the fear of emptiness. We think, "If I give I will have less and therefore feel lack." In contrast, giving is love and is always positive. Giving recognizes our connection.

I have heard of clubs where they get together to perform random acts of kindness. This is giving. This is pure love. It is the natural recognition of our natural connectedness.

LOVE is GIVING

Giving is always positive when it comes to giving time. Giving time means patience, attention, allowing, accepting, listening and tuning into another.

Giving naturally happens when you feel your connection. It's not an effort but a natural process of Being and feeling connected.

Here are the states of giving:

APPRECIATION: You are giving the recognition of another's actions or achievement.

ATTENTION: You are giving your time to pay undivided attention to another.

CARING: Caring is seeing your connection to your brother or sister and therefore is an automatic act of giving.

EMPATHY: It's the ability to feel what another feels because you understand. This is automatic giving of your energy.

HAPPINESS: Happiness is never selfish. Happiness is the natural result of giving. It makes you feel good about yourself. True happiness is love of yourself just as you are. If you give in order to gain, then there is no genuine love of self, and so happiness is a put-on.

In the scriptures, it's given for us to love one another and to love God with all of our heart, mind, and soul. This is another way of saying, give and you shall have.

All taking is a fear of love
Because it is afraid of its own lack.
The egoless law
Give away what you want
And you shall have it forever.
The Universe is a big copying machine
It duplicates whatever feeling you have inside you.

True Love is Emptiness

The word "emptiness" is a powerful word because it leaves us without ground, without a crutch. And that's its beauty. It has no expectations, no ulterior motives and no need to control. Therefore, it's automatically allowing, open and giving.

The most direct way to experience emptiness is to allow yourself to experience the fear when it surfaces (without trying to get rid of it). Suppose you are going to give a presentation, a talk or an introduction. You feel anxious and nervous (which is quite natural). Then instead of feeling bad for feeling bad, welcome it by a momentary awareness that it is just energy. Breathe into it and say, "This is energy, and by allowing it I will be more energetic." And then watch the results and be happily surprised.

Awakening LOVE Through Detachment

Our human state is so hypnotic that we only experience the human emotions rather than the BEING who is Presence of Awareness. The Being is the Spirit-Emptiness that makes it possible to experience our humanity.

What is it that binds us so much that it keeps us on the surface of things?
The answer is a simple one. It's attachment (self-consciousness). We have become so attached to the surface waves that we miss not the ocean depth.

Attachment to the "Me"

Self-consciousness is an attachment to the "me" idea and is itself a "problem." When you see yourself empty and therefore see yourself as a presence of awareness, then the problem of self-consciousness drops away. When you are no longer affected by that problem, you no longer have a problem.

It's a fact that what you hold onto, you will lose. You are empty, but if you hold onto the idea of being someone special, different and separate, then it will produce the opposite effects of what you want most.

For example, the moment a man starts believing that he owns the wife he has already lost her. We cannot own anything without eventually losing it. This is how we learn. Be empty, and in this innocence, you celebrate your life which now has become your love.

The key is loving without attachment. If the wife sees the husband as the provider, then arguments will often happen until separation results. Marriages break up through owning, which is impossible.

This is the paradox: when you are empty, you don't own anything, and so, you have everything. What you try to own, will own you and you'll lose. Move freely in life and in this freedom. You are love itself. LOVE IS EMPTINESS.

In the book, *Enlightened Living*, we read, "Be willing to let go of everything. Anything that is real will remain, but the attachment will be gone. It is attachment that binds and causes pain. Freedom from attachment is joy and leads to the fastest and most comfortable growth. Attachment leads to hell."

How do we know if we are attached to ego?

Review your daily thought-patterns. What percentage are concerned with your survival? That percentage is attachment to your ego.

Why do we become attached?

Because of the superficial value we place on people and objects. We believe that these objects and people will give us what we are missing.

When you allow yourself to be empty, there is nothing missing. Paradoxically, it's through emptiness that we feel complete and full.

You cannot detach from something you still want to be attached to. Acknowledge your attachment whether it is power, fame, sex, alcohol, smoking, drugs or relationships. Write down what you are getting out of it and what will happen if this attachment is removed from you?

What if I am attached to my mate?

Then your love is not free because it's constantly tinged with fear, jealousy, possessiveness and demands. You choke the love out of your partner eventually. The relationship will have to die.

A detached relationship is a holy relationship because when together they are one, not two. There are no ego walls to cling, to possess, to own but merely an expression of melting.

In the book, *You Can Have it All!*, we read, "Noticing the way the Universe functions and using it as a model leads us to conclude that the ideal state is freedom of movement. Air moves freely through the atmosphere. Water flows freely down the river and streams. Waves flow freely onto beaches. The earth moves freely on its axis. So, it is in the affairs of humans. Allowing things to flow freely in our lives gives us the maximum benefit from each experience. One of the ways we interfere with the free flow of energy is holding on to what we already have."

The Fourth
GROUND-BREAKING
Unknown
Fact of
Reality

The Miracle of Trust

The Fourth Unknown Fact of Life is the overall power of trust, which is at the core of emptiness.

Someone asked me, "All these many years you have practiced spirituality, what have you learned."

My answer was direct and simple, "All I have really learned is to trust that which I AM!"

Trust awakens when the truth is seen clearly, "I AM SPIRIT!" It's the safety, security, and freedom we seek all our life but rarely find because it is hidden in the very center of our being—Emptiness!

Here is a simple way of learning the beauty and power of trust. It's a unique way of understanding the mystery that embodies the main teachings of the greatest Masters. What did all the great Masters teach? This is what they all said: Jesus the Christ said, "I am the way, the truth, and the life." (Referencing Christ Consciousness also known as unconditional love).

Krishna said, "Love me, trust me, see me everywhere and think only of me." (Referencing Krishna consciousness or Spirit Being.)

Buddha said, "Everything is Empty, it is nirvana, it is trust. Trust me."

Bhagavan said, "Give me your problems and fears and trust me. I will carry your burdens."

They are all saying trust the Spirit Emptiness that I am and you will experience myself in you.

Let me tell you the story of how the world misconstrues emptiness and makes it something to hold onto. I am reminded of the story of Bodhidharma, who introduced Zen Buddhism into China. The emperor had come to receive Bodhidharma at the border. If he had been anybody else in Bodhidharma's place, the emperor would have cut off his head immediately because he was behaving in an unmannerly way.

The Emperor created hundreds of temples, made thousands of Buddha statues. One thousand scholars were continuously translating Buddha's words from the Pali into Chinese. The imperial treasury fed ten thousand Buddhist monks. He did much to make China Buddhist. Obviously, he thought he would be appreciated. So, he said to Bodhidharma, "I have done these things. What will be the virtue out of all this?"

Bodhidharma replied, "Virtue? You blind fool!" in front of the whole court because the court had come with the emperor. There was stunned silence. The emperor was so shocked he could not speak. Then the Bodhidharma continued, "You are destroying a living word, and you are feeding these scholars who have nothing to contribute to the consciousness of the people. Still, you have the nerve to ask if you are doing a great virtue?"

The Bodhidharma went to the hills just outside China's boundary. Sitting in a temple, facing the wall, he declared, "To talk to people who don't understand is just like talking to a wall. But talking to a wall, at least, one has the consolation that it is a wall. I will turn my face only when I see that somebody has come who is worthy of listening to the word."

Finally, one person did come, and he cut off his hand to prove how earnest he was in experiencing the living word.

What is the Living Word?

The Living Word is the Living Truth. This means there is only one source of all life. It is not only the life-force within the seed; it's not only the energy within the sperm that creates the living embryo; it's not only the force that keeps the heart beating, but it's all the atomic force that creates structure out of itself and allows matter to appear real and solid. It is one source, one energy. Everything we experience, sense, see and feel is this living force. It is emptiness itself! Emptiness is so simple to feel and experience, that when it reaches a point where you can trust it absolutely than that's the great joy of living.

How to Learn to Trust This Emptiness

Feel it out what it means to be empty. It's so simple, and yet, because of its simplicity, we overlook its great importance, much less trust it.

Now imagine this moment to be empty of all past, future, fears, ideas, concepts, self-image and interpretations. Sounds like a tall order but what it's really saying is this: relax completely in this moment as if nothing else exists. You are totally empty here and now. What would be the innermost feeling? It will feel like a COMPLETENESS with nothing needed or wanted, a feeling of utter safety, tranquility, bliss, contentment. It's an inner knowing that everything is okay with everything else. In other words, at the very core of this emptiness is TRUST.

TRUST is a difficult word to define because it's part of LOVE. Actually, trust is a mystery because it's the quality of emptiness. Watch a child's comfort and bliss as she holds her father's hand.

We survive through unconscious trust (instinct). We trust we will wake up in the morning. We trust our beating heart. We trust that the food we place in our mouth is masticated, digested, assimilated and distributed without checking for it.

When unconscious trust is explored and found to be emptiness itself, it becomes the highest love. It's the essential core of love.

No information can teach you trust. There are no courses you can take or workshops and seminars. Trust grows by knowing that emptiness is the source of all things. Just as a wave becomes a particle (Spirit into flesh) so does particle (body) experience the wave through inner emptiness known as Silence and stillness.

Osho said, "Love itself is a mystery and undefinable because it is emptiness. Love is like a circumference and trust is its very center, its soul. Love is like a temple and trust is the innermost shrine in the temple where God is situated."

Ordinarily, we think of trust as faith, it is not. Faith is emotional; it is in something and often sentimental. Faith could be blind, but on the other hand, trust is emptiness itself. Faith comes from belief. Trust doesn't come in belief in anything. Trust in its purity emerges from the realization that love is emptiness and therefore limitless and all encompassing. It is your own growth in experiencing emptiness that awakens pure trust.

For example, you have a fear of a particular person because he reminds you of a past unresolved pain. One day he knocks on your door, and your first reaction is to shut the door on his face. However, this time you remember the inner face that says to you, "Experience this fear." You let him in, for, after all, he has never done anything to you. You allow yourself to experience him. You ask him about his hobbies, his interests, his family, his work, and pets. You see another side of him because you allowed yourself to experience him sincerely. Finally, you also realize that everything you felt about him before was an illusion. It's at this point that you begin to trust him. You do not trust him as a person; you trust because you see there was nothing to fear. The trust has awakened as a result of seeing there was nothing to fear. The more emptiness you discover, the greater the trust. In short, as you realize the emptiness of fear, to that extent you awaken trust.

Two Kinds of Trust

Since trust is at the very core of emptiness, then trust is part of our unconscious life as love is. Therefore, there are two kinds of trust—unconscious trust and conscious trust.

Unconscious trust is what we take for granted. For example,

we trust we can walk, we can talk, we can eat, and the food gets digested, we can feel and experience and sensually perceive things.

We take these things for granted without question. This is all unconscious trust.

Unconscious trust has another facet. It becomes negative trust. Negative trust is inevitable as the result of unconscious trust. For example, the human mind cannot understand emptiness as the living truth. It organizes it into a ritual, a practice and becomes a tradition. The mind doesn't question it, and it automatically becomes negative trust. It dictates your life, takes over your thoughts and creates prejudices, judgments, and interpretations. Before we know what is actually happening as adults, we are caught in a world of illusions, also without questioning. THIS IS NEGATIVE TRUST which creates all our negative thoughts. We now live in certain rules, conditions and demands both in social life, married life and career life. We feel inwardly bound, stifled and without knowing why. This is the negative trust of daily life we have taken for granted.

People listen to the teachings of the *Course*, listen to talks on Advaita or the words of the Masters and still ask questions like:

"But I still have to be human."

"I can't help reacting as I do."

"I know it intellectually but haven't realized it yet."

These questions regarding grasping something so simple as the Living Truth (Emptiness) are raised because of negative trust. We have made the appearance more real than the source that created it. <u>We have made our thoughts more real than our awareness of them</u>. We can even watch a movie on a screen and during the movie we forget it's just a movement of emptiness appearing real temporarily because it reflects on the screen.

All emotional suffering is the result of negative trust.
Our respite from this suffering comes in the form of entertainment, pleasure seeking and worldly pursuits, becoming successful and making something out of our life.

Why do we need to make something out of our life?
Because it's not enough as it is. We don't feel complete. We feel something is missing; something is wrong. Therefore, we think we need to add something to us. This is all the result of negative trust.

So, we are caught in skepticism, greed, overwhelming needs, and desires, competition, fear and separation. Negative trust guarantees failure in relationships because of a deep lack of awareness and daily "sleep" state. These are accepted ways of living because they have become our unconscious trust. It's here that we start to seek for a way out of this misery without grasping the simplicity of what-is (emptiness).

Emptiness is the only truth we need to know but who is there to teach us that?

Why is the teaching of emptiness not widespread when it is so simple to wake up through it?
Believe it or not, the negative trust always chooses to learn information, take courses, listen to self-improvement seminars then get interested in the simplest way to awaken by simply being more aware. After all, what comes first—thought or awareness?

Without awareness, thinking is not possible. With awareness, we can be aware of thought and also able to transcend it. But the negative (unconscious) trust would rather struggle against negative thinking than simply shift consciousness to awareness of Emptiness.

Emptiness comes first because it's the creator of life as we know it just as the wave creates the particle that becomes matter. The wave is emptiness or pure energy.

Jesus, Buddha, Krishna, Ramana Maharshi, including all great Masters throughout history have told us that emptiness (Spirit) comes first—then we master life. And yet, we made the word SPIRIT into "something" and missed the whole point.

This living truth is the scariest of all because it's infinite without a boundary line. So how could the unconscious-trust-mind face it without quivering? The unconscious-trust-mind can't deal with emptiness without a crutch to hold on to, without a name or form. Jesus said, "I am the truth and the life and only through me can you be saved!" This is the Truth "shouted" by every Master and still, the mind had to put form into place before it could grasp its simplicity. Jesus referred to the Christ-consciousness and not his physical name and form. Emptiness is the wholeness, the totality, and oneness of all life from which all creation emerged. Religions were created by man and never a Master. Why?

Humankind needs something to hold, see and feel like material form before he or she can grasp the invisibility and formless of truth known as Spirit emptiness.

When we feel something is missing or feel incomplete, it's because we can't accept the formless invisible truth of emptiness as the highest and the holiest.

Truth is not something studied or learned but DISCOVERED as the very Source of us. It's who we are. Our true nature is infinite and eternal, and it's also fully aware, conscious, and alive a thousand times more than Negative trust in the physical body. I didn't understand such a truth fully until I had my Light Experience and saw and experienced my true ecstatic "form."

Is there an end to negative unconscious trust?

Negative trust is the trust found in the world brought on by fear of emptiness. This fear brings a feeling of negative emptiness, which creates the need for fulfillment. This need for fulfillment is encouraged by millions of courses given on the Internet for empowerment. These courses, although true, mislead people by making them temporarily happy without awakening inner trust in emptiness itself, which is truth. Advaita Vedanta and non-duality teachings cover emptiness but, only very few people who are already mature gravitate towards such teachings. *A Course in Miracles* covers the subject of emptiness but is often misunderstood due to its Shakespearean type of prose. Also, it covers words that are used in Christian literature such as Holy Spirit, Atonement, Christ, etc. These all mean emptiness.

The world is also filled with intellectual skeptics, cynics, and hard-boiled atheists. Yet, they have chosen this path because of negative emptiness, which is unexplored.

The only way out of negative trust is conscious and aware trust by knowing emptiness. A perfect example of living emptiness is seen through a pregnant woman looking forward to her experience of birth despite the excruciating pain of delivery.

The Birth Delivery

Here is the perfect example of awakening trust in emptiness. Picture a pregnant woman in love with her growing child inside her. Picture the child as emptiness for, after all, it was just a sperm that reached the womb and gave birth to a fetus, and then living organism.

Now she experiences the pain of delivery, and she may scream in agonized pain. Yet, she does this willingly knowing this pain of the former emptiness has given birth to the positive emptiness known as a living breathing human child. The moment she holds the child in her arms, she forgets all the pain and becomes in love with the child.

Thus, by allowing the pain of negative trust she now experiences positive trust known as LOVE.

In brief, we turn negative trust into positive trust, or rather, unconscious trust into conscious trust, by giving birth to a whole new way of seeing (the new-born child).

Unconscious trust without looking into it with awareness brings negative trust. This is the birth of everything we do not want.

All negative thinking such as worry, fretting, confusion, uncertainty, fear, anxiety, etc. is born through unconscious trust without awareness.

Unconscious trust means we take for granted the daily miracles of living and breathing, waking up and sleeping, eating and digesting, walking, running, smiling, laughing, enjoyment, and so on are all things we've taken for granted without gratitude for having them. When daily life is taken for granted, then we become unconscious. This unconsciousness leads to the need for pleasure—bad food such as sugars, donuts, candy, and all comfort foods. Over-indulgence in sex brings dissipation of physical energy. Over indulgence in comfort makes us too lazy to exercise and keep healthy. All this unconscious living brings escape, greed, fear, indulgence, addictions, etc.

Whenever there's a physical symptom of discomfort, we rush to the doctor who gives us drugs to kill the symptom without healing the cause. This is what we do to escape discomfort without learning from it and so the negativity increases to the point of almost insanity.

Life is to be consciously experienced in gratitude and love, and then this alone brings conscious trust.

When we allow darkness, we begin to see the light. When

we fear darkness and avoid it, we attract it into our life. This is the LAW OF ATTRACTION. We are the product of what we have attracted into our life. We automatically attract what we think about.

How to Trust Emptiness

As we have already discussed, there are two kinds of emptiness. First is unconscious emptiness that we instinctively fear, and then there is conscious emptiness which, we discover after allowing ourselves to experience unconscious fear.

The term EMPTINESS is a perfect word for it. Most people have called it God and then turned it into a religion and created wars. Many called it LOVE and romanticized it. Many called it "Truth" and worshiped it outside themselves.

The word "empty" is perfect because it can't be defined. It can't be classified or placed in any slot.

Someone complained and said, "I call it LOVE, but I also know that there's so much more and beyond my mind." But, the fact remains that the moment you give it a label, it's the nature of the mind to create a mental picture. The moment it's a mental picture, it solidifies and restricts our experience. All labels are concepts, and they are automatically stored in our subconscious where the LAW OF ATTRACTION makes its play. We may pretend otherwise but our lack of AHA! is obvious.

Emptiness has no labels or concepts but is simply empty of everything. When you allow yourself to be empty, then you are relaxed, open, innocent and always ready to see deeper. Emptiness is infinite beyond any boundary line. Osho, Bhagavan Ramana, Krishnamurti and many other great Masters advocated this: empty yourself of all ideas and LOOK at things in a new way and you will grow like a tree in Spring. You see, there is only

ONE and the moment you make it empty then the possibilities are endless.

Let's look at it from another angle. Let's assume that you are faced with people you know who are suffering anxiety, fear, depression, anger, frustration, boredom, listlessness, etc. Ask yourself this, "What is truly happening?

Go immediately to the word "emptiness," and you'll clearly see that they are suffering from a feeling of emptiness. Why? Because emptiness is the greatest fear of humankind when they DON'T understand it. Unconscious emptiness is truly a gut-wrenching experience. It's the feeling that something is missing; that something is wrong. Basically, it's a feeling of deep loneliness despite appearances of bravado and extrovert behavior.

Negative unconscious emptiness is a deep (also unconscious) fear of being no more. A fear of death.

Please hear this and let it awaken your understanding of its simplicity. It is this: all emotional suffering is a fear of emptiness.

A deep nagging itch that we're missing something and, that something is wrong. It becomes a form of insanity and illness when we try to get rid of it by going to a counselor or psychiatrist who's not awakened to the glory of emptiness. You cannot get rid of this feeling by taking a drug or being counseled to cope with it.

There is only ONE WAY to rise above it, and that is . . . to fall in love with it. Paradoxical, isn't it? No, not really!

It's easy to fall in love with emptiness as any great Master will tell you.

Krishnamurti said emphatically:

"The more you know yourself,
the more clarity there is.
Self-knowledge has no end,
You don't come to an achievement,

You don't come to a conclusion.
Self-knowledge is an endless river."

Krishnamurti is saying that self-knowledge which means knowing who and what you are isn't an achievement. It's not a conclusion. You don't label it, but keep open to seeing more and more. This seeing of more happens when we can take our "suffering" into a whole new perspective by saying, "Here is something I don't understand and it's taking over. I must allow it to see where it takes me."

It sounds scary (but it isn't). Our fear grows the more we try to get rid of it. It expands with every effort to control it. But the moment we allow it by saying, "I'm not listening to what it's trying to tell me," we see it for what it really is—even fear is empty!

If something in your life keeps getting worse, then you aren't listening to its message. Suppose your attempts at fixing an attitude or fear or addiction doesn't work. Why keep struggling, beating your head against the wall?

Find a place where you can relax, take a deep breath, pray for strength, and then empty yourself of it completely. The moment you start to relax into the moment something deep starts to happen, the struggle starts to wind down, and your heart opens to "just being." Soon you will find yourself emptied from that fear of emptiness and moments of clarity start emerging.

You see, you are turning fear into love; negative emptiness into positive and conscious emptiness. In this positive allowing of emptiness, you are fertile; you are ripe for new ways of seeing. You've opened your heart to that which is higher.

A few weeks ago, my daughter visited me after a twenty-two-year absence. The moment she told me she was coming, I felt everything taking place by itself. The moment I saw her at the airport with my dear friend, Candise, it was as if no time had taken place. The reunion was prophetic like a Deja-vu. We became empty of labels such as "my daughter" but simply being with another part of me. Two weeks went by quickly, and we wasted no time enjoying each other.

We did a series of videos titled, "Love talks with the Hardings." Reiterating, in one of them I said without any preparation or plan, "If someone asked me what have I learned in all these years of spiritual service and practice, I would say nothing but awakened Trust in that which I AM."

YES! It is simply this—awakening is trusting the emptiness of this moment known as I AM. It's not a something; it's not an object nor a practice but a BEING HERE as nothing and empty. It's glorious! Emptiness is empty from structured ideas; freedom from the way things-should-be! It is innocence and total allowing because THIS MOMENT is eternal, unending and thus always fresh, alive, spontaneous and unpretentious. There is no past nor future in emptiness. There are no rules in emptiness. There are no fears or conditions in emptiness. Emptiness is like a child laughing. It is the wagging tail of the puppy and the springiness of the kitten in its play. Watch children in innocent play, and you will see emptiness dancing.

How can emptiness do my work?

Funny you should ask this because it's always emptiness which does the work. When I'm writing this, I know beyond doubt, it's emptiness writing.

Emptiness is awakened from its sleep by seeing it everywhere.

When emptiness is unconscious, it creates havoc, wars, insanity, revenge, hatred, anger, malice, and all so-called evil.

Readers ask, "But is it like this?" simply because Infinite Intelligence created humans out of itself so that they can experience the glory of Being. However, humans are born without a memory of their past incarnation and so relearn to walk, talk, speak and experience. In this unconsciousness of emptiness, there's bound to be some suffering simply because we take everything for granted. This "suffering" pushes us to question; to probe and to look at things. It's this "looking" at things that we begin to see the beauty and miracle of Creation. We take nothing for granted such as walking, eating, sleeping, talking but seeing how emptiness does everything through us. This emptiness known as WAVE ENERGY manifests in our life when we start seeing its grandeur. The more we see this wonder, the more we fall in love with emptiness, which we embrace as unconditional love.

After all, can you really know joy without exploring sadness?

Can you appreciate real beauty without accepting nonbeauty?

Can you master emotions by controlling them or seeing their emptiness?

Unawareness of emptiness known as unconsciousness is experienced as unawareness of truth expressed. "I feel empty," and "I feel lost!" "I don't know what I want," "I feel something bad within me."

When awareness of emptiness is seen, and experienced as completely empty like an innocent child's mind, then you say, "I feel full," "I feel happy." "I know who I AM," and "I feel good," without having to say it.

Seeing and Trusting with an Open Heart

A consciously empty mind is one that's not burdened with thought because there is trust. Trust is knowing, without a doubt, that all is God's Laws. These laws are simple because they follow harmony, peace, love and all that is good. Thus, when one consciously surrenders to all that is good, there is no need for effort nor control, but allow. This allowing is called CONSCIOUS TRUST IN EMPTINESS.

The *Course* says, "The teachers of God have trust in the world because they have learned it is not governed by the laws the world made up. It is governed by a Power that is in them but not of them. It is this Power of Trust that keeps all things safe. It is through this Power that the teachers of God took on a forgiven world."

When you see this power, this emptiness, this great void within everything then you've seen God. No matter what the world does to you, you have already forgiven it before you even think about it.

This emptiness requires an open heart to see it. Here are some examples:

You start recording in your camcorder your child's first words, first steps, and all those experiences surrounding it. You feel good about it because you trust that whenever you want to see the videotape, all you have to do is play it in your player. But, now you want to know where this recording is even though you can't see it unless it's played. So you look for the name or number you gave this recording. The video can't show you its recording because what has been recorded is invisible electromagnetic energy. It is the same with audiotape recording. It is the same with computer memory. IT IS ALL-EMPTY and only appears when it "moves" inside a player.

ALL LIFE IS THE SAME! It only appears when it's moving. When energy becomes still, it enters the emptiness beyond its expression and waits for its e-motion to express itself.

The same with us. By having made all emotions empty of negativity and pain, and suffering through consciously learning from them.

So, what have we learned from all our negative emotions by making them empty?

We have learned that all emotional suffering is a search for meaning, love, happiness, peace, joy and all that is good. All we ever truly wanted when we were unhappy was to be happy. When we were lonely all we ever really wanted was to be loved. All we ever wanted when we were desperate, and suffering was to feel complete and whole. However, because we were immersed in so much pain, we expressed only resentment, anger and fear. We compounded our unhappy feelings by making them more needed and desperate.

This is what happens when we directly experience what we are seeking through emotional suffering. We are seeking our true nature, which is emptiness. So, what is emptiness really?

Emptiness is another way of saying all that is good—happiness, peace, love, joy, and all feelings of wholeness.

Test it. The next time you feel miserable, hurt, frightened and so on, take a few deep calm breaths and then enter by seeing this negative movement as a need for emptiness. You don't assume emptiness; you just relax into being here-now (which is itself emptiness). This direct experience may not alter your feelings right away, but having had the inner strength to relax is enough to bring in the power within you in time.

Let Us Repeat the Process

The emotions we feel in our body are experienced thoughts that start moving inside us. When we start looking at them after taking a deep breath, we will discover they are emptiness like the video and audio recordings. They appear real only when they are moving. It's all motion. Similarly, with all matter, it only appears real because of its continual motion.

For example, the body, which we take to be so real, is nothing more than a high frequency of energy in motion. The trillions of cells which comprise the body, are constantly in fever action. To us they appear solid and still.

Physicists know that the body is empty space. All is emptiness.

When we look at a thought, that is, really look at a thought, look at it straight, it disappears because it was never there until it moved. The moment it moves, we have an impression. When we believe it's real, then we feel its e-motion through the body. If we react believing it's real, then our belief makes it seem real, and we suffer. However, our belief and suffering are both emptiness.

Our stillness in the LOOKING eliminates the "movement" and shows us its emptiness. This is permanent healing. It's all simple, and we need not pay loads of money to someone who can teach you to cope with the pain. LISTEN TO YOUR OWN POWER. Save your money and be your own guide. Let your Spirit-Emptiness be your teacher.

Asking one more time, "What is the very nature of Emptiness?"

The very nature of emptiness is LIGHT. Light is unconditional love experienced during an NDE. It's Infinite Intelligence; the Source of all living things. It's timeless, beginningless and endless. It is also known as Spirit, Being, Holy Spirit and God. The word "emptiness" is the most appropriate label since the third-dimensional linear mind can't understand it any other way. When fully empty of thought and bodily concern, you are close to the Light."

The great Master Wei Wu Wei asked, "Why are you unhappy? Because 99.99% of everything you think and everything you do is for yourself, and there isn't one."

That's why the word "emptiness" to the human condition is so appropriate.

The famous Chuang Tsu said, "To a mind that is still and silent the whole Universe surrenders. The Spirit is an emptiness ready to receive all things."

A famous saying goes," Because I live in Absolute Absence, I AM the eternal Presence."

The *Course* says, "In your world when you hear the word 'Course,' you think of learning. But you are not here to learn. You are here to EXPERIENCE. And you will find with great joy, that there is a dramatic difference between the two."

The Paradox of Truth

The word that depresses and frightens us the most is the word "emptiness." Yet, when explored and understood, it becomes your very savior.

All evolution of consciousness follows similar steps just like the child learning to walk and falls a few times in the attempt. So is our expansion of consciousness follows the experience of emptiness as fear itself, only to discover the gem within it when allowed to be fully and directly experienced.

Fear is not a fact. Fear is the illusion humankind needs to rise above pettiness to find his glory in the very thing he feared.

F.E.A.R. means False Evidence Appearing Real.

LOVE, wholeness, Reality, Being, God cannot be known by the limited mind. The mind is merely a small fraction of the total consciousness. The mind only knows its own creation but never that which is beyond creation such as emptiness. Therefore, any attempt to understand or know with the mind isn't only futile but leads to frustration, confusion and even insanity itself. However, the word "emptiness" although fearful to the mind can also bring the point that Truth is beyond mind. Thus, when the mind is empty such as the gap between thoughts, it's here that starts the discovery beyond mind.

A Quantum Jump into Healing

The best way to understand "The Four Facts" is by knowing that all material form has emerged from pure essence. That is, first there is energy, then it moved in waves; waves give way to particles; particles into atomic structure; to molecular structure and finally into matter. Thus, matter emerged from nothingness (no-thingness). This is the duality of human existence.

Human existence (not knowing it's a Being) first) is driven by a need for gaining, having, belonging, owning, even accumulating. The drive for having is a need for experiencing love, happiness, and peace.

When happiness is not found in "things", then it seeks knowledge. Knowledge information then becomes another accumulation—the need to know, the need to be smart, shrewd, worldly, clever.

A time will come when wisdom and intelligence replace cleverness, smartness, and shrewdness. This brings the awareness that awakening to life is not a gaining of things but a release, letting-go, surrender and trusting the Source from which everything emerged. However, the need to know through books, literature and wise words are sought and become another form of seeking. This seeking for happiness through words is natural in the beginning making believe that reading wise words help to create a wise heart. However again, this accumulation of knowledge/information doesn't mean happiness and heart meaning. When this dichotomy is understood, then there is the wisdom to awaken to Spirit essence.

At this point, we begin to understand through the heart that our true nature is the very Source of Life. It is our true Being. It is "gained" not by the accumulation of information but by inner freedom from gaining and owning.

Summarizing The Four Unknown Facts of Reality

a. The Source of all Life (existence) is EMPTINESS without form. Its nature is Infinite Intelligence and expresses through unconditional love.
b. It gives no rules nor commandments but FORGIVENESS. The term "Emptiness" of form defies explanation or definition.

Emptiness without form is the nightmare of the human who, as yet, hasn't realized that one's true nature is Spirit.

All human suffering is emotional. Emotional suffering is all due to the fear of emptiness without form such as fear of death; fear of losing something; fear of not being good enough; fear of not knowing what one really wants, and so on. Therefore, this simplifies all psychology why there is suffering of depression, anxiety, guilt, and fear. *Repeating, all human emotional suffering is a fear of emptiness.*

Take the case of the close-knit relationship between a mother and daughter. One day the mother decides to visit her father whom she has not seen in quite a few years. She has a good time with her father and although her daughter misses her, yet she reconciles it with just missing. The more the daughter hears how much her mother is having a good time with her father, the more the daughter misses her mother while stifling and suppressing thoughts of jealousy (quite unconsciously).

When the time comes for the mother to arrive home again,

the daughter had suppressed her feelings so much that she bursts into unwelcoming anger toward her mother without both realizing what is truly happening. The mother, in turn, is thoroughly upset over the reception. She blames herself, unconsciously, for not being a good mother. Suffering follows without understanding what actually happened. This kind of emotional suffering is the SECOND UNKNOWN FACT. Suffering is unrecognized love awakened through forgiveness.

All human suffering stems from the fear of emptiness such as missing someone or feeling less-than or comparing, etc. This suffering is also known as Emptiness without form as the cause of suffering.

Great attachment to physically feeling good could result to addictions whether sexual, intoxication, or over-emphasis on the body one way or another. Fear of death is one of the most common fears.

This SECOND UNKNOWN FACT is all human pain when there is no recognition that one is not a body but a SPIRIT with a form.

The SECOND UNKNOWN FACT is transcended when the love of Being Spirit is meditated on and results in conviction. Suffering only ceases when the realization dawns that one is a formless Spirit still endowed with full awareness. And, it's in this realization that full awakening happens. What is it that happens when there is full realization one is a Spirit in human form?

There is the recognition that only LOVE WORKS, and there is only LOVE!

c. True Love is emptiness without form. For example, you love a song or musical piece so much that you dance to it with total expression. In this case, there is emptiness because you are one with the music. There is no ego need.

True love is forgiveness of self since FORGIVENESS is Unconditional Love and all suffering are lessons where love hides itself only to be discovered. Another example is when a pregnant woman gives birth. The moment she holds the child in her arms, she is empty for only the child exists in her attention.

d. Wisdom is born when there is total trust in Emptiness, which is Source itself. This TRUST through forgiveness has awakened acceptance of the daily miracles of life such as heart beating, breathing, eating, walking, talking, laughing and the ever-miracle behind all known as Pure Awareness. This awakens acceptance, love, gratitude and joy in full living.

Here is how to learn to trust emptiness and awaken love. The next time you are suffering emotional pain such loneliness, feeling not being good enough, a self-esteem issue, frustration, fear of death, and so on, take a deep breath acknowledging how you are feeling without trying to fix it.

Then ask yourself, "What form of emptiness is frightening me?"

Loneliness seeks a partner; depression seeks to fill a void by doing something; anxiety is a fear of a missing something in the future. In other words, all emotional suffering is a fear of emptiness or losing something. Taking a breath, allow yourself to see that you are throwing away a chance at love by fearing it. The emptiness you fear is truly love itself when recognized. It is this that will bring transformation from fear to love of Self. There is only LOVE!

Lessons from Emptiness

As Candise and I were having lunch at Aphrodite's, she expressed to me the perfect picture of Emptiness—watching a young Indian girl in India, eating a watermelon. The relish, joy and total immersion in her eating pleasure left nothing to be desired. In expressing this to me, I also witnessed Candise in that state of emptiness.

Emptiness is the completion of the moment as a total here-now bliss which is the very nature of Being. This emptiness is perfect love. It is Being One with what-is.

A week ago, I watched a *Britain's Got Talent* video in which an unassuming young girl appeared on stage to sing. The moment she began to sing a hush spread over the huge theater. Tears were visible in the judges' eyes. She captured the entire several-hundred-people audience in rapture with her voice. The reception was so captivating that everyone was standing and clapping in delirious joy to her song. She WAS the song, and everyone became one audience in that Emptiness.

Emptiness is a fullness where the personal is lost as it becomes one with the moment. This is love.

When the Emptiness is seen as a lack, then, the personal becomes needy for love instead of being-love. This seeking of love is the suffering, the guilt, shame, fear and hungering for what we already are but don't know it.

Frequent meditation brings us to that Emptiness which is the fullness of Being. Being is always full because it's itself the one consciousness known as unconditional love and so it's infinitely intelligent.

How to Meditate

Meditation is very simple. Just sit comfortably with your back straight and head erect and simply watch your breath. Start by conscious breathing and then simply follow it naturally for a short while.

Soon you will begin to feel Empty from the personal to the fullness of Being. Play some soft relaxing music and enter that Silence. It is that simple. The ego will resist initially, but soon regular practice will become a joy. Ego literally hates emptiness and tries to fill the moment with things to-do and think. In Silence, even the third eye becomes enhanced to the point of sheer joy.

Start with five minutes daily and build up as your emptiness dictates.

A Quantum Jump into Healing

This Quantum Jump will only take a few moments to bring healing, but it requires a full understanding of the Second Unknown Fact which is fearing emptiness.

This is how to take a Quantum Jump in three steps:

a. If you are suffering from any problem, stress or uncomfortable situation then take these simple steps. Use it as a learning-device to take you deeper into "knowing." Meditate on the feeling of fearing Emptiness without form. When you see it clearly what is happening . . .
b. Visualize it as a fear of emptiness while allowing the experience to happen. Forgiveness is automatic. Click the finger of the right hand ten times slowly while fully experiencing the stress without indulging in it.
c. Return to normal acting "as-if" you are now healed. The more convinced you can imagine yourself healed, the quicker and more lasting the result. Remembering all suffering created by the fearing emptiness is really an illusion of the mind that had created a habit pattern.

Questions and Answers

Could you give a brief and succinct explanation of the FOUR UNKNOWN FACTS OF REALITY?

Keep in mind that all FOUR are ONE called EMPTINESS.

If you keep Emptiness in mind and "see" everything from that perspective, that's clarity also known as peace, wisdom, and joy.

1. The First Unknown Facts says Emptiness is the only TRUTH. The reason it's unknown is that it strikes fear in the heart of humankind and therefore it's avoided. Religions were organized by man with rules and conditions to control Truth which is really impossible. Krishnamurti made it clear that Truth is a pathless land.
2. The Second Unknown Fact lets us know that all fear and guilt, all negativity and emotional suffering are the result of fearing emptiness, mostly commonly known as the fear of death or being no more.
3. The Third Unknown Fact is understanding that Emptiness is LOVE itself without limit. It's unconditional love, which the heart wants without knowing it. Just like the child who is constantly being yelled at by his mother for being difficult when all he wants is, "Please love me as I am and not as you want me to be."
4. The Fourth Unknown Fact of reality is TRUST in Emptiness where all glories and Heavenly gifts come from.

In these FOUR UNKNOWN FACTS OF REALITY lie all psychology, psychiatry, counseling, metaphysics, philosophy and all unnecessary learning when all is needed is the experience of emptiness as the Light of Being. Emptiness is also called God.

The word trust means surrender, reliance, prayer, allowing, relaxing, being still, entering silence and so on.

What is the most important thing to understand about the Four Facts?

It is the #1 major force and energy of the Universe. The other three are its expressions or manifestations.

The obvious way to understand this one greatest force in the Universe is to know you are a human Being.

A human is a form and its' BEING is the Truth known as EMPTINESS. It's empty of all form and expresses as BEING ("to be") here-now; beyond time; allowing, accepting, letting-go and forgiving. It's all there is known as unconditional love and expresses as Infinite Intelligence.

Are there many kinds of LOVE?

There is only one kind of love which is the emptiness of self and immersion into the Light. However, humankind understands love through degrees of caring—physically, mentally, emotionally and finally spiritually. It takes many, many lifetimes to awaken full unconditional love. We first learn it through loving another, and then it spreads until there is only LOVE. When love becomes one's true expression, then wars cease, quarrels diminish, fears drop away, guilt is wiped out, and heavenly joy becomes the daily experience. There is no end to love and its deepening.

Osho says that love starts horizontal such as before and after known as emotional love (often tinged with fear and hate).

Then it becomes vertical where the only way is up, up, up.

Is love what we are here on Earth to experience?
We live simply to discover Love! It's through love that we experience full emptiness and thus real heavenly joy.

Why do we need to experience our fear first before we know love?
Can you really know joy without knowing sadness first? Fear and suffering teach us the most when we allow ourselves to experience it directly. Love is your true nature which needs to be discovered by meeting fear head-on with compassion.

My favorite example of this is the mother bearing a child in her womb. Delivery is often met with suffering, and yet the moment the child is held that's the blossoming of love.

When fear is avoided and pampered, then it increases until the whole organism collapses either through chronic illness or simply giving up life.

Fear and suffering need to be experienced without taking drugs to deal with physical or mental symptoms. The healing of fear and suffering is the healing of the mind that tries to avoid, escape and pamper (play victim).

Is love then experienced as fear from the human point of view?
True love is the emptiness and depth of Being where everything appears as one. This is the greatest fear of the ego that tries to placate fear and suffering with victim-mentality. Fear and emotional suffering are great lessons in themselves, and they only happen as we create them. Suffering doesn't happen by chance but by our own hand. Once we start seeing this clearly and take responsibility, then experiencing them directly is the key.

Taking drugs to placate symptoms can lead to great physical danger such as heart, kidney, and other collapsing organs.

I have an issue with the word 'emptiness.' If emptiness is love, why not use the word 'love' instead?

First, see how subtle the ego is not to accept the word empty. Why do you fear it?

The ego has a field day with the word "love" when it's not fully understood. The moment we label anything, we begin to have an image of it. The moment you have an image of love, then you become stuck and unable to transcend it. To keep expanding in love is to see it first as empty of definition because it's too grand, too powerful a word to play around with without grasping its immensity.

Love is emptiness. However, the word "love" can only reveal our emotional concept of it. Love has no limit, and that's something the mind cannot even begin to understand.

You said that all fear is fear of emptiness. Love is also emptiness. How are the two the same?

First of all, there is only emptiness, and there is nothing else. Emptiness means empty of all objects and things. Empty refers to utter and absolute inner Silence. It's inner tranquility. It's the joy of the child where thought has not gripped him yet. What seems to be other than emptiness is the appearance of emptiness known as matter. You see, all matter whether it's buildings, ground, bodies, houses and so on are all matter that was produced from emptiness. The wave became a particle and then became solid structure. However, all matter is emptiness because it's made up of atomic energy, and bodies are cellular energy. All are empty as scientists point out.

The moment the mind becomes tranquil, silent, still, then it starts to feel love. For example, you take your child for granted, and one day you are both sitting still together and, one glance at the child suddenly makes you realize how much you love him.

Oneness is love as the true nature of everything. It's the oneness of energy since we are all one same energy. First, you allow yourself to experience emptiness, and then through that emptiness, you go deeper than form and recognize that "person" beyond their looks. It's here that you actually start feeling love.

When you recognize how much you have been running away from emptiness, it's then that you start awakening your love capacity.

If doubts, uncertainties and ordinary daily stress are fears, how are these a fear of emptiness?

In order to grasp this great truth, one has to get in touch with the two drives—the drive of emptiness for its expressions such as the need for peace, tranquility, connection, oneness, warmth, bliss, wholeness, joy and inner fulfillment. Then, we have the drive of the ego. The ego drive is to experience the qualities of emptiness such as love on its own terms. The ego is the personal self that is often trying to protect itself through arguments and disagreements, safeguarding itself. Thus, it narrows down beauty and love to its own selfish expression. After all, that's its nature.

Now, the moment the ego becomes addicted to its selfish ends, it develops pride, greed, manipulation and control. When it starts losing its control, like a child who lost its toy, it develops doubt, uncertainty, and stresses. A co-dependent relationship is an example of personal selfish love that wants control. How does it feel when its control doesn't work? It feels insecure, doubtful, uncertain, fearful. In other words, it feels empty. This is the fear of emptiness. This negative feeling of emptiness is equated with feeling lost.

So, in truth, everything is empty. Isn't that discouraging, disheartening and even depressing?

It depends upon who's thinking it. To the ego, it definitely is depressing. To one who sees clearly, it's a celebration. It's the most beautiful truth.

Remember, things are not going to get empty. They are already empty, have always been empty, but not seen as such when the individual mind believes the form is all there. Recent scientific discoveries prove that everything is empty. Physicists know everything is empty. What we see as material form has emerged from emptiness. Once this is realized, then, there is the knowing that LIFE is ongoing. LIFE may be seen through a living form, but the moment that life is withdrawn then all that's left is a lifeless shell. All of our senses, aliveness, the beating heart, circulation, digestion, distribution, and so on and on is all energy in motion. Thus, all is empty until it's energized into motion.

What makes an ego is a strong identification with name and body. It believes wholeheartedly that this is the self. In truth, all is consciousness appearing real through motion of energy. The more you believe you are just a body, the more you suffer because everything is based on the superficial values. This mentality robs the ego from knowing the deeper and more beautiful love-life.

When the ego becomes lost or desperate, then it's a matter of how it handles this drama. It can either drive the ego into insane behavior or, it can make it realize the truth of emptiness.

We are here on earth to evolve, and so we have to wake up one way or another. There is no other choice. The ego believes it has many choices, but in point of fact there is only one choice—either to continue trying to control your stress through drugs and will-power which often leads to breakdown, or, choose the aware state of how things are.

Matter is mass, atomic energy. Atoms are empty. Our bodies are 99.999% empty space.

What is enlightenment?
Enlightenment is the full awakening into the fact that everything is empty known as Spirit.

Do material things change to our view when we see them as empty?
Viewing through the physical eyes is the same for everyone. However, when one awakens to the truth of emptiness, then the sensitivity of seeing with third-eye is enhanced. Thus clairvoyance makes one see beyond matter into Spirit.

I remember how after my Light experience in the hospital I began to see Spirits and even auras at times. When I meet someone sensitive to emptiness, then I can feel their aliveness. I still see Spirits often. My cat who passed away after eighteen years began visiting me after his passing into the Spirit world. I tried photographing him to show Sivia (my ex-wife who loved him), but I had no success.

What happens when you wake up?
Nothing extraordinary. You are the same as before except that now you appreciate beauty, feel more grateful for being alive, happier and more at peace. Things don't bother you anymore like they used to. You are no longer attached to people or things, but yet have a greater capacity to love deeply.

You discover water when all around you people are thirsty (understand my meaning?). Waking up is coming to your senses while still in a mad house. You laugh easier and more often because you don't see anything worth worrying.

Is self-confidence an ego trip?
Self-confidence emerges as you allow yourself to see everything as empty. Seeing emptiness everywhere increases self-love which

has nothing to do with ego but merely feeling a greater sense of connection and oneness.

There are so many courses that teach empowerment. Are they necessary?

Courses in empowerment are good, and they even make you feel good about yourself. However, the results don't last unless there's the actual recognition that everything is empty. Emptiness is a beauty like the child's eyes and smile.

What makes a flower beautiful and awesome; what makes a mountain powerful and gives you a sense of freedom? What makes music so energizing? What makes poetry so heart-wrenching? All these things are empty, and that's their awesomeness. Emptiness is beauty in motion.

How does guidance emerge from emptiness?

Real guidance is inner guidance, and it always comes from inner Silence. For example, let us say you have a problem or a question you need solved and can't answer it. What do you do? Enter the quiet abode of your Being. Relax completely both physically and mentally. Listen to your breathing until thoughts become unimportant like clouds across the sky. Then after a while start watching how emptiness is breathing you. Talk to emptiness saying something like this, "My limited mind doesn't know the answer to this problem. I give it over to you until you show me the answer through emptiness itself."

When I said in a video of mine, "In all the years I have been doing spiritual work and service I haven't "learned" anything but awakened trust in Spirit." Many Internet viewers asked me to clarify it in a simple way. During the night, I was awakened by an energy that told me to write down the points received. Still, in a drowsy mood, my hand wrote, "There are Four Unknown

Facts of Reality" and now you are reading this material. All of it emerged from trusting emptiness.

What if I have no trust in emptiness?
That's okay, that's why I've written this book. Actually, you're already ahead of most people simply because you know you don't trust emptiness. Now, it's a matter of reading this book until it all comes naturally to you like it did for me.

Can you explain how clarity and trust are the same?
What is clarity? It's seeing things as they really are! In other words, it's seeing the truth as it is. For example, have you ever looked at the intricate wonder of a flower, a leaf or a spider's web? Aren't you then filled with the love and intelligence of emptiness that created it and you? When you are filled with wonder, don't you trust it? Trust sees what-is clearly. Trust isn't something you do. It's what awakens when you allow yourself to look at the obvious miracle of life!

I identify totally with my body and self-image. How can I experience the state beyond the body?
You experience the state beyond body when you experience the body fully. For example, every fear experienced alters our breathing rhythm, our body temperature, our glandular secretion and so on. When you experience fear—STOP—pay attention to your breath. Feel the different physical sensations. Give them space to do their stuff. Eventually, you will realize the body is energy moving with every emotion. It is the physical manifestation of thought. This awareness makes us realize the body is moving energy of space. In other words, the body is emptiness appearing real from that motion. Every emotion is e-motion (energy motion), and it's this motion, in the world, that makes matter appear real.

What level of awareness do we need to reach to recognize the body is emptiness?

It's the 5th stage of awareness called body-awareness stage. These stages, although sequential ordinarily in their growth process, don't necessarily take time. One could jump from one stage to another in seconds, or it may take a whole lifetime. The reason these stages seem to take time is because of the slow deprogramming of our ego control, self-sabotage and the resistance to experiencing emptiness.

The Seven Stages of Awareness Growth

The following are the seven stages of awareness growth. This will give you greater patience and compassion towards yourself. The moment you fully accept where you are, then the next stage will be that simple and even easy.

1. Survival Orientation: This is a very materialistic viewpoint. The world to you is real and solid. No questions are raised, and there is no seeking yet for expansion.
2. Seeking Answers: There is the desire to be somebody. A need to improve, be better, gain more knowledge. Some seek even religion at this stage or some belief system.
3. Heart: This is when you place importance more on the heart than the mind. Feeling more rather than knowing just knowledge and information.
4. Detachment: The first glimpse of awakening. This is the Direct Approach to truth rather than following a system or belief. You know you are more than a body. Your interest is focused on the Spirit within. In this case, emptiness is understood.

5. Body-Awareness: This is when you recognize that the body is an appearance and not the truth of Being. This is considered an advanced stage.
6. Here-Now: This is the recognition of timelessness and that the truth is in this eternal now-moment. The awareness of infinite intelligence and contact with it.
7. True Self: This is living from the true Self by continual awareness of it in daily life.

How does knowing these FOUR FACTS awaken all knowing in the heart?

These Four Facts are actually ONE TRUTH known as emptiness. The moment you start experiencing the truth of Emptiness, you will feel the insight of Infinite Intelligence. This Infinite Intelligence is the Spirit of Truth known as God or Holy Spirit or simply Divine Light of unconditional love. It works this way—the moment you recognize emptiness, just like in deep meditation, you will actually feel the Spirit of Truth like a dear friend whispering in your ear.

What about the Soul?

The Soul is the very emptiness itself, the invisible divine light of Being, the part in you that has never known beginning and will never know end. It will journey throughout eons of so-called time from one life to another until these FOUR FACTS are fully lived.

Jesus said, "In my Father's House there are many mansions." This means that our growth, evolution, expansion or whatever you want to call it, is ever drawing you towards itself. The potential glory is endless.

For thirty years, I have been a hypnotherapist with much success. I was thrilled by clients telling me about their past lives and their evolution. That is, what they have learned through their many lives and what else is there to discover. I chose the name SuperSentience as the name for hypnotherapy which I will soon take up again.

SuperSentience means using the FOUR FACTS for deeply exploring the many mansions of the soul (dimensions, levels, etc.).

If Love is Empty, then there is no one who is doing the loving, is that correct?

That's correct! When your heart is full because it's empty of ego, then guidance is ever with you step-by-step.

Emptiness means knowing you are Presence of Pure Awareness and not a body alone (as most people believe). This love ushers forth from you like water from a tap because you FEEL the Oneness through emptiness of ego.

What can one do to evolve faster?

This is where trust comes in. This emptiness is itself a trust in the divine Infinite Intelligence, which is everything. This TRUST alone will take care of you without your attempts and efforts. After all, through awakened trust, there is a voice that is ever with you and guiding you.

Can past lives help us to heal faster by seeing lessons we still need to discover?

Yes! When you enter stillness (emptiness) then your soul memory takes over and remembers. This remembering can happen through the aid of a hypnotherapist or by yourself from deep meditation.

Can you give me an example?

I had a woman come to me who was desperate for an answer to her constant stomach pain. She was in her forties, and her pain never stopped. Sometimes she would throw up her food from the pain. She visited doctors, psychiatrists, psychologists and no one helped. She came to see me as her last resort when a friend happened to mention my name. This was a few years ago.

Talking to her revealed that she didn't believe in past lives and was also born a Catholic. I didn't promise anything and told her so.

I had her lie down on my bed and started relaxing her with the idea in mind that we will trace back the source of this stomach pain. Suddenly, within ten minutes or so, she started screaming, "Get off me you bastard!"

I was a little taken back because I didn't want the neighbors to think I was doing something nasty.

She kept screaming and then she twisted as if a huge pain penetrated her stomach and she went silent, almost unconscious. I gave her a command to remember what happened and started awakening her by counting backward from five.

She opened her eyes and looked in shock. She didn't say a word but looked dazed. Finally, after I gave her a glass of water, she started getting up but retained her dazed look. I gave her space to talk if she wanted to but didn't.

Finally, after about half-hour, she got up feeling dizzy. I asked her, "How do you feel?" referring to her usual stomach discomfort. She reported, "It's gone, my pain is gone."

Apparently, what happened was a brutal rape followed by being knifed in her stomach.

Later that week she sent me an e-mail explaining how her life has changed by knowing she lived before, knowing that her religious upbringing wasn't true and life on earth was evolution of Soul towards the One True Love. She visited me, and I took her to lunch. She was a completely changed woman. She was humorous, pain-free and happy even looked much younger.

Since emptiness means fullness, why not use the term fullness instead?
No one initially likes the word "emptiness," and that's why it's so effective. Your question clearly points out how the word isn't favored. Anything else you use other than emptiness will eventually lead to a hold in evolution.

For example, most people love the word LOVE and use it often. What usually happens is that they stop evolving in that love. Why? It's the nature of the mind to create mental images. Mental images create a structured inner picture which solidifies, and so, further growth about love becomes stifled. After all, you have created what LOVE looks like. This is how the ego was created—through a self-image that became real.

The Founder of Psycho-Synthesis said at a group meeting, "95% of your energy is spent protecting, defending and maintaining your self-image, which is ego, and it is nothing more than an image."

The word "emptiness" has no rival and no definition. It's the best word for Spirit, God, Truth, Love, and Oneness.

Why? Because emptiness leaves you empty without an image and therefore your subconscious remains clear. Thus, when there's no self-image, then there's endless truth without a boundary line. Expansion follows naturally. When you fall in love with the beloved Emptiness, then you can actually feel your oneness with the Divine Light of Being.

I am beginning to see that emptiness is the highest freedom!
It's the only true freedom from conception and play of words. Jean Klein, the well-known musicologist and enlightened teacher said that it was after his enlightenment experience of emptiness that he fully grasped the meaning of physical intimacy. This, he attributed to the awareness of pure energy.

How can you know what stage of awareness you are without being prejudiced?
It's not difficult if we are honest. The stages are quite clear-cut. Simply put first we see the physical as solid reality, then we start seeking when not happy with just material form. Seeking leads to confusion and hard questions and even fear. Then through meeting that fear and confusion, we start becoming open to possibilities beyond words. After all, words are concepts. After that, we start maturing by understanding that the only fear was emptiness and by getting to know it, we were led to freedom and clarity.

I get it! By knowing how much we hate the word "emptiness," we also get to know its ever-present beauty!
You got it! By knowing why something truly irks you, also leads to knowing its power over you. By knowing why you hate it also awakens you to that previously-obscure knowing.

Why is emptiness superior to all thoughts and emotions?
Thought is limited to the past as is emotion. Also, thought cannot go beyond itself, neither can emotion. So, since emotions can't go beyond the emotional feeling, one is faced with the clear evidence that one can never attain the unattainable. You give up personal effort and clearly see how you were holding yourself back by your fear of emptiness. It's through this "seeing" (which is not easy) that surrender happens, and grace brings you to the more advanced stage.

So, one does his/her best work by actually doing nothing!
Since everything is empty, all we can do is allow ourselves to be empty. This means all we need to "do" is observe ourselves as we "try" to improve or be better. Ask anyone over fifty if they ever tried to do better and improve and most all will reply that they

have tried. Look and see if they've found spiritual fulfillment, peace, and inner freedom?

Emptiness is fulfillment. It's LOVE beyond concepts as the whole. It isn't achieved but awakened to through observation of how things are. All we need is awareness through looking at what-is!

How does emptiness bring such Universal Intelligence into our Being?

It doesn't bring Universal Intelligence into our Being. Emptiness itself is Universal Intelligence. It's the void that created you and created all matter out of itself. It's PURE CONSCIOUSNESS. We can't understand it any more than we can fly physically. However, we can grasp the magnificence of emptying ourselves and becoming instruments of the universal flow. We can only KNOW to the extent that we empty our minds from "trying" to know.

Sit very still, take a few deep breaths and relax completely. Start becoming aware of thoughts and watch the gap between them. It's this very pure awareness between thoughts that knows the illimitable. Start by asking yourself a very deep question that very few people know the answer, and then ask it of the Inner Silence. The answer will come to you in an unexpected way as an inspiration.

How can we experience truth in total honesty when we don't know what truth is?

That is correct. Truth is not something that we can deliberately feel or experience; it's the constant awareness of non-truth that can reveal the truth.

For example, how can you be aware of truth? It's by knowing that truth is empty and has no qualities. Thus, the very awareness of a thought is what makes awareness the truth and not the object it's aware of.

Suppose you become aware of yourself being aware. This awareness of awareness is the truth and NOT what you are aware-of!

When you feel love towards someone, the truth isn't that love, but the connection of everything you feel. Truth is like a bottomless pit that arrives nowhere and therefore everywhere. This is why the word "empty" is so appropriate for further recognition of truth.

Therefore, is truth the very miracle of each moment as it happens when there is no ego?

That's right! Every moment is empty which means it is full of meaning. Go out into the forest and see how everything is talking to you whether it's the tree, the air or just the flowers that seem to have a life of their own.

How can I feel the word EMPTY?

Just look around you without naming anything and see their energy of aliveness. When something is empty, it means it has no way to define it because it's ever moving energy appearing so real. Hold a flower or leaf in your hand and really look at it without making up your mind what it is and see how grand its Creator is. How did it come into being? How did the fertile ground produce such beauty?

Next time you feel the wind in your face, talk to it. When you listen to the waves beating against the rocks, listen to their music. When you gaze at the stars at night, let your heart swell with wonder without reaching a conclusion. It's this very awareness that brings the glory of truth closer to you. Truth is also here-now when you see with emptiness.

Awareness is itself the miracle of existence, the Presence of Being and the evolving love of nature.

So, the truth is awareness itself?
YES! It is the ever-present undying part of you. It is your very Being without end. It's who you are eternally. And, as we fall in love with awareness we will understand what EMPTINESS means. Awareness always IS!

What is the difference between consciousness and awareness?
They are different and yet one eternal whole. Awareness is the emptiness that created all living things out of itself like a spider weaved a web from itself. Awareness is pure known as Pure-Awareness. It is the truth and creator of all life. Then Awareness wanted to experience itself because it knew no boundary line, no limitation. It was as if PURE AWARENESS (God) was thinking, "I want to create a form out of my own Light so that it can evolve and experience my glory."

Thus, the Soul was a beam of Light that wanted to experience itself through form. It was like saying "When awareness became aware of the first thought, consciousness took place. Consciousness, says the *Course*, was the first split in Creation.

It began to create form from itself. Thus, everything became consciousness, and the world took shape. However, it had to limit itself from the truth such as having TIME and SPACE into it so that form could be visible as if real. Thus, bodies were created when time came into being. The brain was created with its linear understanding to work the body. Humankind could not experience its Soul completely in the body, so started from scratch. This limitation made the body subject to time, and so it was constantly changing until the time came to change bodies again through rebirth.

To keep the body alive meant continual care for food, shelter, and exchange of energy. Humankind believed it was that very body and so created an ego from that image to name and form. It was this that brought hardships and suffering.

Awareness and consciousness were completely one and survived beyond form. When humankind became aware of this SOUL, it became ripe for awakening. Awareness and consciousness never separated, so death was impossible except for the body which only appeared real.

So, when we become aware of our consciousness and its content of conditioning, is it, then we awaken to the truth and never forget it?

As we become aware of our consciousness, which is the content of our thoughts, emotions, and beliefs, this awareness expands until we realize who is being aware. It's awareness itself which is being aware. It is like saying God is seeing God. This is the enlightenment.

So really, when we talk about emptiness we are really talking about this fullness of consciousness and becoming aware of it!

That is the whole journey on earth. The word "emptiness" leaves the mind free from concepts and images. It prevents the mind from playing games by thinking it "knows." This is why great human beings were innocent like Jesus, Bhagavan Ramana Maharshi, Ramakrishna, Osho, Buddha, Krishnamurti, etc.

So, which is it that produces suffering in the world? Is it the emptiness we fear or the seeking of our Spiritual nature?

Seeking Truth through the mind is suffering confusion, frustration, perplexity and the agony of never "getting-there."

However, the real suffering is brought on by the fear of emptiness in practically every case. Fear of emptiness (due to unawareness) is fear of death; fear of not making it as a human being; fear of feeling lost; fear of being no more; fear of not being good enough and so on. Usually seeking follows our fear of emptiness such as addictions to drugs and drinking; addictions to sex; addiction to negative thinking; not knowing what you want, etc.

The moment you realize that the very FEAR of emptiness is a contradiction because emptiness is what is needed to awaken. So, the game is this: we are afraid and running away from the very thing we need and want above everything else.

When our search is finished, is that the end of the journey?
There is no end to the journey as there are no limits to the glory, splendor, and beauty of which we are heir.

How are worry and concern fears of emptiness?
All negativity is a fear of emptiness—even doubt and dislike are fears of emptiness. The way to rise above that fear is the willingness to stop and LOOK at the fear, feel the feeling beyond the label "fear" and really get to know that feeling. When you feel empty in a negative way such as bored, listless, unhappy, and so on then acknowledge the fear. Sit with it for a few moments while experiencing to discover why it feels negative. After all, what is the meaning and feeling of negative? Isn't it a feeling of discomfort without knowing why?

Look at it, not as something wrong but a search for meaning. Talk to your Being as if praying, "I am feeling so bored or restless or fed-up or uncomfortable and so on." Then say, "I give this feeling to you!" which becomes a form of trusting the emptiness. If you really mean to do this "practice," you will actually experience emptiness not as negative but rather positive within an hour or so. The more often you do this, the more often you gain power over yourself. That's what a Master is—he or she has mastered oneself.

What makes the experience of emptiness so ecstatic and beautiful?

Ordinarily, it's the fear of emptiness that creates emotional suffering. The more we try to get rid of it, the bigger it gets until we become sick physically, mentally, emotionally or spiritually or all of them.

When emptiness is embraced, there is innocence and glory following that allowing.

Did you ever watch talent shows when the particular person was appreciated for their talent with applause and cheering?

How did that person feel? At that moment, they felt so empty that they disappeared as a "person" and became totally egoless, even quite humble and sweet. The love and attention bestowed on them were unexpected, and the result was euphoria of great joy. All ego disappeared, and the emptiness was sheer heaven.

Does enlightenment mean the total disappearance of personal identity?

No, of course not. You are a unique human being and shall always remain so even after physical death. What makes you so rich inside is the love and trust you have of emptiness which is impossible to describe until you feel it.

Is the freedom from fears and negativity that which creates the high feelings?

It's more than just the freedom from fears. It's the feeling of Presence. You feel connected and in love. You feel love for all because you know, beyond a doubt, that it is all one being. There are no longer strangers—there is only "us."

How can one live from emptiness when there are things to be done?

This is a common question, and it shows that there is belief in the power of ego-doing. This is such a hard-core belief that it takes many attempts at explaining and answering questions before the mind grasps something so simple.

Let me ask you again, are you keeping yourself breathing? Are you making sure that your hair keeps growing? Do you keep your heart beating? Do you make sure your blood is circulating? Do you check to make sure that your food is digested, assimilated and eliminated properly?

Everything worthwhile is done by "Being" (emptiness itself).

Now let's assume that you have a job to do, which requires creative thought. How do you go about it? Ask yourself, "Which is easier, fretting over it or giving it over to your higher consciousness (emptiness)?"

You see, when we do something with love, then love will do it through us. The body simply acts through that love automatically and perfectly. When creative thought is necessary, then the clarity will be present.

To answer your question directly, when we live from emptiness, then everything gets done more smoothly, more efficiently, in much less time and energy consumption.

There is still the thought that if I'm empty I'll become a moron, a simpleton!

You are just expressing the fears of the ego, that's all. Be aware of the question you ask because that will reveal what you are aware of. Ask yourself this, "Was Jesus a simpleton? Were the great Masters morons?"

Emptiness is the only real intelligence. It created not only life in the Universe, but it also created the brain.

How did Einstein create the theory of relativity? How did Beethoven create glorious music when he was deaf?

We could keep going with examples, but you get the point. It all emerged from Emptiness.

What happens to the daily mind when it becomes empty?

Then it functions at its optimum because the Universal Mind will take over. The fact is, there is no individual separate mind, there are only thoughts that make up one's reason, intellect, memory, deduction, logic, and mental function. Real intelligence is when we hook up with Emptiness.

Picture the personal computer that can only function according to the software and the programmer. But, then hook it up to the Internet, and you have access to virtually unlimited knowledge. So, it is with us. Our individual mind is limited to our past conditioning. When it's empty of content, then we are hooked to the Universal Intelligence.

Emptiness isn't a vacuum; it is an incredible mind-boggling intelligence.

I did not come up with the Four Unknown Facts of Reality in this book, they were inspired by higher Source, and I was the instrument to write them.

Is emptiness of ego mind something we learn to do? I'm still not clear how to achieve mental emptiness?

You don't achieve mental emptiness. Thoughts never cease coming into your mind. You simply realize that everything is empty. The moment you clearly see that everything was and is empty, your mind follows suit. It's not something you do. It is something you realize as already the case. In other words, we wake up to what already is!

I have read this book, and although it touched me deeply, I still can't seem to live it. It all remains intellectual. What can I do?

It is not something to achieve or try to get. The language and terms used are "new" to you, and so we try to figure them out. This is normal and natural. Be aware of this. Make sure to STOP every time there is an attempt to figure it out or even try to understand. This attempt brings immediate confusion or the thought, "This is intellectual to me, and I can't seem to live it."

Your position is to LISTEN and live it, that's all. The ego might ask, "How do I live it?" that is to be expected. Observe the constant "figuring out" of the ego to keep you from experiencing and living in the moment.

This is "how" you do it. Become very still, very still and relaxed. Observe your moving breath for a few minutes. You may keep your eyes open. Just look forward slightly above eye-level and FEEL how everything is a movement of energy. Observe our moving body, heart beating, breathing; the different subtle sensations of your body such as its weight, stomach activity, if any, and so on. Notice also the movement outside of you such as the clock, cars outside, and any activity. Everything is moving energy. JUST BE AWARE without judging or figuring out. FEELING PURE AWARENESS!

This WATCHING or observing of what-is begins to awaken your knowing of what you are. You will begin to realize you are the AWARENESS of the constantly changing panorama. You are not the panorama. You are the intelligence of the Universe itself. YOU JUST ARE!

If your willingness to experience is earnest, then this "practice" will bring you to a knowing beyond words. You will begin to hear these FOUR UNKNOWN FACTS in a new way.

Is emptiness the very Intelligence of Life?
Absolutely! The term "emptiness" is a perfect word because it deprives the intellect of making conclusions about it. Emptiness can't be conceived by the mind. It might try to think that emptiness is a vacuum, so be alert to this thought. Just keep reminding yourself that emptying the mind from all activity is to invite the Intelligence of the Universe into you. It's through this non-activity of mind relaxation known as Alpha-state of Being that Albert Einstein "discovered" the Theory of Relativity. It's how David Bohm, the Pulitzer Prize-winning physicist, realized the Universe as a holographic image.

The daily mind, although useful in conducting daily routine tasks, is helpless and hopeless in understanding the depth of its own creation—emptiness! Emptiness is pure consciousness beyond concept, beyond memory. It created the memory and brain out of itself.

If emptiness is the Intelligence of Life and everything is created from emptiness, what is that 'something' in the emptiness that creates?
Albert Einstein said, "Everything is emptiness and form is condensed emptiness." Of course, by condensed emptiness, he meant molecular structure, atomic energy that "appears" as matter. In the same way, Buddha said, "Emptiness is none other than form, form is none other than emptiness."

When did Creation begin or did it begin at all if timelessness is the very essence of Life? Can the mind understand timelessness when its very basis is linear time?
Emptiness by its very nature appears as the world. So now the question we are asking is, is it the emptiness that makes it appear as matter?

Emptiness is pure energy. It's beyond comprehension.

Scientists know of it but can't understand it either. Why? Because IT JUST IS! After all, in truth there is no time, so how can the mind fathom that?

Scientists only know that the electron within the atom behaves in a seemingly erratic manner and cannot be understood. However, whatever it creates is intelligent. It knows what to do. It knows how to create a heart, kidney, an eye, brain and so on in the fetus. We can call it memory. The moment energy "moves" it is memory moving. For example, in technology, we know that electricity activates memory and we have audio and visual phenomena. A recorded tape can have a talk or movie embedded in it. When the memory is activated through the tape player, it comes to life. Similarly, when the computer is off, it's just dormant energy. There is nothing there. When it's powered on, the memory signals are activated and it "remembers" again.

The body acts much the same way. Our body is moving energy. The body never stops moving, unlike the computer. The body is circulating the blood keeping the heart beating and so on and on. It's this continual motion of energy that makes it seem alive. When we sleep, the body is very active such as breathing, etc. Cell changing moves so fast, its perfection blows the mind. If this motion ever stopped the body would disappear into dust. The body is an appearance of emptiness (pure consciousness).

There are three principles to energy (the Holy Trinity). First, we have pure emptiness, the great void of pure consciousness. Then we have memory or activity of energy. Third, we have the appearance of form (the world of matter and form).

Are emotions the memory of the body?

Your body remembers, and this remembering is the e-motion (energy motion). If the memory is tinged with judgment, then it becomes negative emotion. Judgment is based on ignorance of our true nature. All "bad" experiences are judgments made by an unconscious reaction. In the overall scheme, there are no bad experiences. There are only just experiences to "learn" expansion of love (emptiness). Nothing happens by chance in an intelligent Universe. Therefore, whatever happens is "something" we need to look at with greater compassion, freedom and knowing of our natural love nature.

Some people have more love in their life than others, is that because they deserve it more?

In an intelligent and perfect Universe, there is no such thing as deserving of love. LOVE IS EMPTINESS ITSELF and so always present! Some people have more love because they know they are empty of ego. People who experience more love are people who claim it as their very nature.

In other words, love in your life doesn't seem to be there not because you don't deserve it but because you expect it through guilt of some kind. When you know you are empty of ego then love is constant. In truth, there is nothing but love.

So, if one just stops thinking about it and lives moment to moment knowing there is emptiness of ego, then everything is taken care of?

Yes. Life is intelligent and therefore caring. Remember you are emptiness appearing as YOU! There is only emptiness, and it is pure love simply because it's empty of ego. It is more loving than your wildest conception. All it asks of you is trust that you are empty of ego. Trust is intelligence, and it makes you devoted towards it, and you are free.

Is that why the teachings of Jesus, Buddha, Rama, Krishna, and all enlightened Masters mentioned surrender?
Surrender is not something you do but naturally happens when TRUST is awakened. One doesn't surrender but simply remains empty of ego.

Can you tell me again what is ego?
To make it simple, it is this: ego means that you believe you are just a body/mind organism and so believe you are your self-image. The truth is that you are Presence of Pure Awareness (emptiness). When the belief is that you are a separate individual made up of the past conditioning, then you are naturally resisting of emptiness. The ego (personal self-idea) based on the belief you are the past conditioning, you are filled with negative thoughts built from it. Ego wants to be in control and so gets easily angered and upset. It wants to know that it knows and so is arrogant and often closed-minded. Ego wants love on its own terms and so is often a failure at love relationships. Ego is easily attached when it can't have what it wants. And then when it has it, grows tired of it.

With emptiness, which is so simple, there is no ego because you are completely here now with what-is as IS!

Is it then a matter of becoming more aware of emptiness then?
Exactly! Ego is a lot of work and is often either moody or easily upset and hurt. Whereas, the emptiness from ego is relaxed and goes all along with everyone and everything as is.

Keep remembering emptiness as your real nature of love, joy, happiness and fullness of aliveness. People who are empty always look younger than their years.

Is keeping awareness of emptiness moment to moment a place of love, bliss and joyous living then?
Definitely! The capacity to love is equivalent to your capacity to be empty.

How does it work then?
Emptiness means just that; to be empty from superfluous baggage. When you are here now empty then automatically love takes over. You see, love is always present and all it needs is the emptiness in which it can flow and express. If there's ego, you have built a wall based on conditioned values and beliefs thus creating a barrier to innocence, peace, love, joy and full living.

Tell me this, why do I find this emptiness you speak of so hard to grasp when my intuition tells me it's so very simple?
Emptiness eludes you because you still are not clear what you want most in life. Everyone wants the same, believe it or not. We all want to be happy, loved and loving, the fullness of life, energy and good relations. Again, believe it or not, you are already these qualities inside you, but you block them through self-sabotage.

Self-sabotage says, "I don't deserve love for I am bad or think too many bad thoughts, etc. In other words, you may carry guilt-feelings of a subtle nature. Guilt feelings always look for self-punishment, believe it or not. This self-punishment is self-sabotage. Did you ever hear people say, "It is too good to be true!"

Most people don't love themselves because deep down they believe they are bad or not good enough. This is hogwash! You have been born a part of God (goodness, love, and joy). Your true nature, when left uninterrupted, is always good. "Bad" people are not born that way but "become" that way through environmental influences. Our heart yearns for "goodness" simply because it's that way, naturally. Your true nature is LOVE and emptiness keeps it that way.

Keep emptying ego every moment you think a negative thought. This emptiness of negative thoughts is also known as forgiveness.

Once you see, even minutely, that emptiness is whole, complete and all encompassing, then you will have it as your focus. This will be your fulfillment.

When I listen to you speak, I feel so good inside, and I resonate with you. So why do I raise so many 'buts,' 'what-ifs,' and doubts?

That is the nature of the ego to sabotage itself. This sabotage, to repeat, is the belief that you are not good enough as you are, and so, unconsciously create barriers to prove this fact. This is the insanity of the ego. When you start seeing how you are working against what you want most, then, this very recognition will be your saving grace. The mind is conditioned by the world's negative trust.

Why is there so much negative trust?

In the third dimensional world of opposites, we learn negative before we awaken to the positive. The world is born from duality. Duality is not real but seems real. Everything has an opposite to make the world function and appear real.

Emptiness became matter through the motion of energy called "wave." The wave became a particle and eventually into a molecular structure known as matter. Matter and Spirit became opposites. Time and space existed to make the world appear real and solid and so living in time and space became limitation, fear, insecurity and belief in death simply because matter always changes form. Every front has a back. Every up has a down and white had to have black. The world of matter, therefore, is the limitation where we learn compassion, love, and trust all over again. However, since the very nature of Being is love, joy, and fullness, then we can only express those natural qualities when we allow emptiness to take over our feelings.

What is the one thing to keep in mind?
It's all one action known as Love, and there is no "other" that can oppose it.

Why are there so many mistakes, suffering, and ignorance in the world?
It is the unawareness of love as Emptiness!

Why is Emptiness perfection when it's nothing?
This is the great illusion of humankind, which is as yet, unable to see that it's the invisible Spirit that is the major mover in the Universe of form.

If form is unimportant why do we need it?
The formless can only gain wisdom through direct experience which can only happen through the form.

What is the real power of the formless emptiness?
It is the only real power. It is the source of energy that created everything from itself. First as energy; then as a wave of intelligence and infallibility; finally, to particles and materiality.

What is wisdom?
It is the inner knowing of how things work.

How do they work?
Through Love which is often mixed up with just an emotional feeling. Love is vast and wants to give, share, enjoy and care without limit. It's unconditional love.

If all is the result of love, why is there hate and fear?
Fear and hate are not opposite love. They are the result of seeking, needing and wanting love without understanding it.

Is there such a thing as someone incapable of loving?
It seems as if there is when the world has not expressed it to the individual. Then it shows itself as the need for power. It's the need to control and get its own way.

Why does lack of love lead to the need for power?
There is only one power in the Universe known as unconditional love. It is the one focus. The power of unconditional love stems from knowing its own Oneness. It wants to give, empower and enjoy itself. When this oneness is unknown due to identification with the form, then separation-thinking seems to occur. Thus, this unawareness of oneness leads to separation thinking. However, the need to empower itself is still strong, and so it strays into the need for control, manipulation, greed, owning, possessing and war to keep winning.

So, is one lost when this power to control takes over?
No, because direct experience in human form will prove that power over another (separation) leads to destruction especially of itself.

Are we now talking about evolution of the species?
Yes! All evolution teaches us that only Love works.

What happens when we realize only love works?
Then we forgive and thus get back to the enlightened state of unconditional love.

Can humankind completely destroy itself?

No! Just as there are ignorant people; there are also many awakened people, and thus balance is always maintained. The force for good is greater than any ego.

What is an ego?

It's the unawareness of the true nature as Spirit. Therefore, I see how Emptiness is Spirit and all negativity is fear of Emptiness believing it's something lacking.

How does healing happen?

It's by allowing oneself to see that all suffering is unawareness of love as the one truth. Thus, fear is the illusion of needing, wanting, craving love on its own separative terms.

Where is God in all this?

God is the emptiness of form and appears as our Light of unconditional love and infinite intelligence.

How do I transform fear into love?

It is quite simple really. Allow yourself to see that fear is a distortion of seeing emptiness. To the intelligent awake human, love is complete and full thus representing the emptiness of form and fullness of Being. On the other end, to the unaware and unawakened human, Emptiness appears as a lack and so feels inadequate, unfulfilled, insecure, frightened, due to egoic belief in the form.

Now I see how we need the form to evolve into our glory?

Yes! We reincarnate to get this lesson right. Our true Home is the glory of unconditional love that even its conception blows the egoic mind away.

“Nothing real can be threatened.
Nothing unreal exists.
Herein lies the peace of God.”

A Course in Miracles

About the Author

BURT HARDING, founder of the Awareness Foundation in Vancouver, Canada, offers a radical invitation to recognize the truth of our being as already whole and fulfilled.

He reminds us of the love we really are beyond the personal stories we carry. In this way, we come to recognize what we have always known but did not live from—the beauty and wonder of our own true essence.

Burt conducts sessions and workshops in SuperSentience; a system devised to help heal deep wounds and promote a shift in the perception of who we really are.

He has conducted studies in higher consciousness for thirty years and had his own television series on the mind/body connection.

www.BurtHarding.com

Other Books by Burt Harding

HIDING IN PLAIN SIGHT

by Burt Harding

Burt Harding offers a radical invitation to recognize the truth of our being as already whole and fulfilled. He reminds us of the love we really are beyond the emotions and personal stories we carry. In this way, we come to recognize how beautiful we really are in our essence. Through Burt, perfection unfolds as it lovingly embraces and lifts you, the reader, to a higher state of consciousness.

THE PERFECTION OF AWARENESS

by Burt Harding

Imagine your heart warm and open, your spine pleasantly tingling. As you look, the colors are brighter, the sounds clearer, like you are truly experiencing your surroundings for the first time. This is how you'll feel when you release the holdings of your conditioning. You'll discover the sacred, the radiant, beautiful awareness of presence everywhere you look.

THE FIRE & MYSTERY OF AWARENESS

by Burt Harding

Pure awareness and consciousness are vastly different and opposites. Once there is a clear-cut understanding of the difference then, and only then, comes the very recognition that will bring an awakening to the truth of our Oneness. Containing the "missing link," this book is about finally awakening to the Presence you are and always have been.

THE TRUTH THE WORLD DOESN'T WANT YOU TO KNOW

by Burt Harding

IF YOU FEEL STUCK . . . Or just need answers, what you seek will never be found out in the world. Burt Harding lovingly offers you the bridge necessary to make the final transition to the fullness of your true nature that answers the question, "Who am I?"

THE WONDER OF YOU

by Burt Harding

What we identify as one Being is a composite of what humans would perceive to be two separate beings. One is physical and the other spiritual—the human ego and the Light Being. What you are about to read will free you from the shackles of fear. You will be given proof by your own discoveries.

Printed in the United States
By Bookmasters